WHAT'S WRONG WITH THIS PICTURE?

Butcher's Blend
Dog Food

Let's see. There's a butcher [cou]nter. With butcher's [me]at. And Butcher's [Ble]nd.® brand DOG FOOD

Butcher's Blend? [Th]at's a dog food.

Right. A delicious [do]g food with a com-bination of 3 of the butcher's meatiest flavors: beef, bacon and liver.

You'll know Butcher's Blend come from a but[cher's] counter. But d[on't] tell your dog.

PLEASE DON'T BOTHER THE BUTCHER.

Better Homes and Gardens®

FAVORITE

MEAT

Recipes

© Copyright 1985 by Meredith Corporation, Des Moines, Iowa.
All Rights Reserved. Printed in the United States of America.
First Edition. First Printing.
Library of Congress Catalog Card Number: 84-62093
ISBN: 0-696-01535-8

BETTER HOMES AND GARDENS® BOOKS

Editor: Gerald M. Knox
Art Director: Ernest Shelton
Managing Editor: David A. Kirchner
Copy and Production Editors: Marsha Jahns,
    Mary Helen Schiltz, Carl Voss, David A. Walsh

Food and Nutrition Editor: Nancy Byal
Department Head–Cook Books: Sharyl Heiken
Associate Department Heads: Sandra Granseth,
    Rosemary C. Hutchinson, Elizabeth Woolever
Senior Food Editors: Julia Malloy, Marcia Stanley,
    Joyce Trollope
Associate Food Editors: Barbara Atkins, Linda Foley,
    Linda Henry, Lynn Hoppe, Jill Johnson, Mary Jo Plutt,
    Maureen Powers
Recipe Development Editor: Marion Viall
Test Kitchen Director: Sharon Stilwell
Test Kitchen Photo Studio Director: Janet Pittman
Test Kitchen Home Economists: Jean Brekke, Kay Cargill,
    Marilyn Cornelius, Maryellyn Krantz, Lynelle Munn,
    Dianna Nolin, Marge Steenson, Cynthia Volcko

Associate Art Directors: Linda Ford Vermie,
    Neoma Alt West, Randall Yontz
Assistant Art Directors: Faith Berven, Harijs Priekulis,
    Tom Wegner
Senior Graphic Designers: Alisann Dixon, Lynda Haupert,
    Lyne Neymeyer
Graphic Designers: Mike Burns, Mike Eagleton, Deb Miner,
    Stan Sams, Darla Whipple-Frain

Vice President, Editorial Director: Doris Eby
Executive Director, Editorial Services: Duane L. Gregg

Senior Vice President, General Manager: Fred Stines
Director of Publishing: Robert B. Nelson
Vice President, Retail Marketing: Jamie Martin
Vice President, Direct Marketing: Arthur Heydendael

FAVORITE MEAT RECIPES

Consultant: Robert E. Rust

On the cover:

Orange-Vegetable Pork Roast (see recipe, page 33)

Our seal assures you that every recipe in *Favorite Meat Recipes* has been tested in the Better Homes and Gardens® Test Kitchen. This means that each recipe is practical and reliable, and meets our high standards of taste appeal.

*Whether you're an expert or a beginner
at cooking meat, you'll find a wealth
of useful information on the following pages.
In addition to recipes, chapters provide information
to help you identify the cuts you see
at the store and explain how to cook a particular
cut of meat. You'll also find
a special guide for buying, storing,
and carving meat.*

Roasts from the Rib

The rib bone, shaped somewhat like a curved "T", determines the name and appearance of rib cuts. Since the meat is derived from supporting muscles along the backbone, it is among the most tender and desirable.

Beef Rib Roast Select bone-in (2 to 4 rib bones) or boneless roast. A solid round of meat —the rib eye muscle— identifies the cut. Commonly called standing rib or prime rib. *Roast.*

Veal Rib Roast is cut from the rib or rack and resembles a beef rib roast, except it is smaller. A **Rib Crown Roast** is 2 rib sections sewn together in a circle with the rib bones on the outside. Either roast may be frenched. *Roast.*

Steaks and Chops from the Rib

Steaks and chops include a rib bone unless they've been boned or cut from between the ribs.

Beef Rib Eye Steak
Boneless cut from the rib eye muscle. *Broil, panbroil, or panfry.*

Veal Rib Chop Resembles a beef rib steak. *Braise or panfry.*

Beef Rib Steak Consists of the tender rib eye muscle and usually the less tender rib cap muscle on top of the eye. Cut about 1 inch thick. *Broil, panbroil, or panfry.*

Since beef is too large to be handled in one piece, the carcass is cut into sides, quartered, then divided into wholesale cuts as shown. Veal cuts are smaller and lighter in color. For specific meat cuts, check the following identification and cooking information.

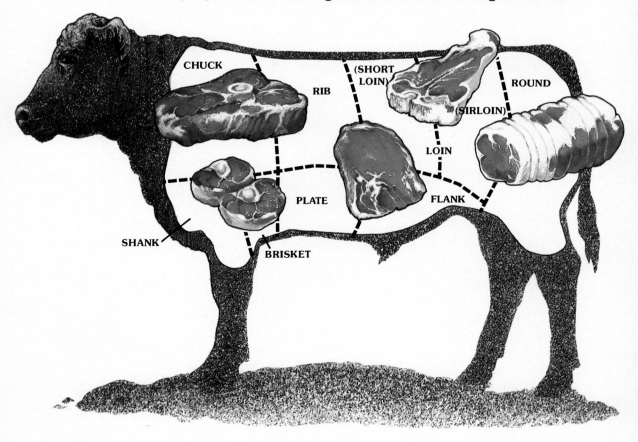

CHUCK RIB (SHORT LOIN) ROUND (SIRLOIN) LOIN PLATE FLANK SHANK BRISKET

Ribs

Rib bones are covered by alternating layers of lean meat and fat.

Beef Short Ribs

Can be cut from the plate or chuck, or the ribs immediately below the rib steak section. Short ribs from the chuck usually have more lean meat than the others. *Braise or cook in liquid.*

Beef Plate Spareribs

Come from the same section as plate short ribs, but the rib bones are cut longer and are generally less meaty. Usually sold in long strips that can be laced accordion-style onto a barbecue spit for rotisserie grilling. Spareribs also come from the chuck, but are called Flat Ribs. *Braise or cook in liquid.*

Beef Rib Back Ribs

Actually the rib bones removed from rib steaks or roasts. Generally well-trimmed of fat and meat and separated into individual bones. Often labeled ` Finger Ribs. *Braise or cook in liquid.*

Veal Breast Riblets

Cut from ribs in the breast section. Fairly lean. *Braise or cook in liquid.*

Roasts from the Chuck

The blade bone or arm bone identify cuts from the chuck (known as the shoulder in veal). The activity required of the shoulder muscle makes the meat less tender.

Beef Chuck Arm Pot Roast

Oval-shaped cut about 2 inches thick having a cross section of the round arm bone. *Braise.*

Beef Chuck Blade Pot Roast

Contains a cross section of blade bone (the bone resembles a reverse "7" near the neck, and a flat blade next to the rib). *Braise (roast high quality).*

Veal Shoulder Blade Roast

Resembles a beef blade pot roast. *Braise or roast.*

Veal Shoulder Arm Roast

Similar to a beef arm pot roast. *Braise or roast.*

Boneless Beef Chuck Eye Roast

A cut obtained by boning the meat adjacent to the blade bone. *Braise or roast.*

Beef Chuck Cross Rib Pot Roast

Rectangular piece containing 3 chuck ribs plus the meat that lies across them, hence "cross rib." Really little more than 3 large meaty short ribs hooked together. Commonly called Boston roast or bread and butter roast. *Braise.*

Steaks and Chops from the Chuck

Chuck steaks and chops are identical to chuck pot roasts, except thinner.

Beef Chuck Blade Steak

Many muscles interspersed with fat and connective tissue. Cross section of blade bone. *Braise.*

Boneless Beef Chuck Shoulder Steak

Cut obtained by boning the meat near the round arm bone. Often labeled boneless shoulder cutlet. *Braise or panfry.*

Veal Shoulder Blade Steak

Similar to a beef blade steak. Sometimes called a shoulder chop. *Braise or panfry.*

Beef Chuck Arm Steak

Includes a cross section of the round arm bone. May be labeled Swiss steak or round bone steak. *Braise.*

Veal Shoulder Arm Steak

Resembles a beef arm steak. Sometimes called round bone chop. *Braise or panfry.*

Meat from the Brisket

Comparatively thin, less tender muscles and fat in alternate layers. Includes plate in veal; called breast.

Beef Brisket

Long flat piece having thick layers of lean meat with little fat. Can be processed for corned beef brisket. *Braise or cook in liquid.* (Some brands of corned brisket can be baked.)

Veal Breast

Frequently marketed as a roast for stuffing. *Braise or roast.*

Steaks and Chops from the Loin

A cross section of backbone or hip bone identifies loin cuts. The loin is the most naturally tender portion of the animal.

Beef Tenderloin Steak Boneless steak, 1 to 2 inches thick, cut from tenderloin muscle. Often called filet mignon. *Broil, panbroil, or panfry.*

Beef T-Bone Steak Contains a section of backbone commonly called a T-bone because it resembles the letter "T." Muscles include the large top loin or loin eye muscle and the smaller tenderloin muscle. Cut from the short loin between top loin and porterhouse steaks. *Broil, panbroil, or panfry.*

Beef Top Loin Steak Small steak cut from the short loin section nearest the rib. Consists of the top loin or loin eye muscle. Also known as club steak, New York strip, and Kansas City steak. *Broil, panbroil, or panfry.*

Veal Top Loin Chop Similar to a beef top loin steak. *Braise or panfry.*

Beef Porterhouse Steak Resembles a T-bone steak in muscle and bone structure except the tenderloin muscle is larger. Comes from short loin section nearest the sirloin. *Broil, panbroil, or panfry.*

Veal Loin Chop Slice from the full loin, usually about 1 inch thick. Similar to a beef steak from the short loin. *Braise or panfry.*

Beef Sirloin Steak Bone and muscle structure varies throughout the sirloin section. Slices nearest the short loin (pin bone steaks) contain the tip of the hip bone. Flat bone sirloin steaks contain the widest section of hip bone. Just behind these are 1 or 2 steaks with a round or oval-shaped bone. Slices nearest the round contain a wedge-shaped cross section of hip bone. For all practical purposes, however, it is necessary to remember only the name "sirloin." Muscles include the top sirloin muscle and the tenderloin muscle. *Broil, panbroil, or panfry.*

Boneless Beef Top Sirloin Steak Slice of the top sirloin muscle with bone removed. *Broil, panbroil, or panfry.*

Roasts from the Loin

Meat from the loin is generally considered to be the most tender available. Usually sold as steaks rather than roasts, except for the tenderloin.

Beef Tenderloin

Long tapering muscle that extends the full length of the loin (the thick end of the tenderloin is in the sirloin). Usually comes with outside cartilage still around the muscle. *Roast or broil.*

Veal Loin Roast Consists of the entire loin section. *Roast.*

Ground Meat

Usually made from lean trimmings and the less tender and less popular cuts of meat. Grinding the meat makes it more tender.

Ground Beef Meat from the flank, shank, plate, and chuck is commonly used for grinding into ground beef. *Bake, broil, panbroil, or panfry.*

Ground Veal Made from any cut of veal. Sometimes sold as a combination package of ground veal, pork, and lamb. Presently no attempt is made to define *or* limit the fat-to-lean ratio. *Bake, broil, panbroil, or panfry.*

Meat from the Plate

The plate area, which includes the ends of the rib bones, contains a high percentage of bone in proportion to meat. Although short ribs and skirt steaks may be cut from the plate, most of the meat is boned and ground or cut into stew meat.

Boneless Beef Plate Skirt Steak Actually the diaphragm muscle. Often sold trimmed, flattened slightly, rolled, and skewered. *Braise, broil, panbroil, or panfry.*

Steaks from the Round

Contain cross sections of leg bone. Fat and connective tissue separate four distinct muscles.

Veal Cutlet Cut from leg; often tenderized mechanically. *Braise or panfry.*

Veal Leg Round Steak Resembles a beef round steak. Tip muscle is included. *Braise or panfry.*

Beef Round Steak Large oval cut with a cross section of the round leg bone. Leaner and less tender than loin steaks. The 4 muscles are the top (largest), bottom, eye, and tip (which may or may not be present). *Braise or panfry.*

Beef Top Round Steak Most tender cut of round. *Broil, panbroil or panfry.*

Beef Bottom Round Steak Sometimes includes both the bottom and eye muscles. *Braise or panfry.*

Beef Eye Round Steak Small oval muscle. Often sold as breakfast steak. *Braise, panbroil, or panfry.*

Beef Round Tip Steak Sliced from large end nearest the sirloin. *Broil, panbroil, or panfry.*

Beef Cubed Steak Mechanically tenderized meat from round or chuck. *Braise or panfry.*

Roasts from the Round

The characteristic shape of the top, bottom, eye, and tip muscles identifies cuts from the round (the same area in veal includes the sirloin and is known as the leg).

Beef Top Round Roast Consists of the single large top round muscle (most tender part of the round). *Roast.*

Beef Bottom Round Roast Consists of the single bottom round muscle. *Braise (roast high quality).*

Beef Round Tip Roast Triangular-shaped cut from the area where the round meets the sirloin. *Braise (roast high quality).*

Beef Eye Round Roast Consists of the small cylindrical eye round muscle. *Braise (roast high quality).*

Veal Leg Round Roast From the tip and center portion of the leg; contains a section of leg bone. Often called leg of veal. *Braise or roast.*

Veal Leg Sirloin Roast The full sirloin portion of the leg. (Section is also cut into steaks.) *Roast.*

Beef Round Rump Roast Includes the top, bottom, and eye round muscles. A boned, rolled, and tied roast is often labeled rolled rump. May come with bone; called a standing rump. *Braise (roast high quality).*

Beef Heel of Round Boneless wedge- or triangular-shaped roast from the lower portion of the round. Contains considerable connective tissue. *Braise or cook in liquid.*

Meat from the Flank

The flank area contains fairly coarse muscles. Most flank meat other than flank steak is sold as ground beef.

Beef Flank Steak Thin, oval-shaped boneless cut with many long muscle fibers and little fat. Often scored to shorten fibers.

Also called London broil. *Broil or braise.*

Meats for Soups, Stews, and Kabobs

Beef Round Cubes for Kabobs Boneless lean cubes of meat cut from the tip portion and heel portion of the round. *Braise or broil.*

Veal Cubes for Kabobs Boneless lean cubes from the leg. Cubes may be threaded on wooden skewers and sold as city chicken. *Braise.*

Beef Shank Cross Cuts Cross-sectional pieces cut from the shank bone, usually 1 to 2 inches thick. During simmering, the tough connective tissue softens and becomes more tender. *Braise or cook in liquid.*

Veal for Stew Cubed shoulder meat. *Braise or cook in liquid.*

Beef for Stew Lean meat cubes cut from the less tender areas, such as the chuck, round, and plate. *Braise or cook in liquid.*

Beef Soup Bone Section of arm bone, fore shank, or neck bone containing little or no meat. Sometimes called marrow bone or knuckle bone. *Cook in liquid for soup.*

Rolled Flank Steak

1 10-ounce package frozen chopped spinach
1 beaten egg
1 cup herb-seasoned stuffing mix
½ teaspoon minced dried onion
¼ teaspoon pepper
1 1- to 1½-pound beef flank steak
1 8-ounce can tomato sauce with chopped onion
¼ cup dry red wine
¼ cup water
1 tablespoon cold water
2 teaspoons cornstarch

● Run hot water over frozen spinach in a colander for 5 minutes or till thawed. Drain spinach, pressing out excess moisture. In a bowl combine egg and thawed spinach. Stir in seasoned stuffing mix, dried onion, and pepper. Mix well.

● Pound meat with a meat mallet to about ¼-inch thickness. Spread spinach mixture atop steak. Roll up steak jelly-roll style, starting from long side. Secure with string.

● Place the stuffed steak roll in a 13x9x2-inch baking pan. Stir together the tomato sauce, the wine, and the ¼ cup water; pour over the steak roll. Bake, covered, in a 325° oven about 1¾ hours or till the meat is tender.

● To serve, transfer meat roll to a serving platter; remove string. Skim fat from pan juices. Stir together 1 tablespoon cold water and cornstarch. In a saucepan combine cornstarch mixture and pan juices. Cook and stir till thickened and bubbly. Cook and stir 2 minutes more. Spoon tomato sauce mixture over meat. Makes 6 servings.

Standing Rib Roast with Yorkshire Pudding

1 4-pound beef rib roast
4 eggs
2 cups milk
2 cups all-purpose flour
1 teaspoon salt

● Place meat, fat side up, in a 15½x10½x2-inch roasting pan. Sprinkle the meat with a little salt and pepper. Insert a meat thermometer. Roast the meat in a 325° oven for 2 to 3 hours or to desired doneness (see chart, page 13). Remove the meat from the roasting pan. Cover the meat with foil; keep warm.

● Reserve ¼ cup drippings in roasting pan. (Or, pour 2 tablespoons drippings into each of two 8x1½-inch round baking pans.) Set aside. Increase the oven temperature to 400°. In a mixer bowl beat eggs with an electric mixer on low speed for 30 seconds. Add milk; beat 15 seconds. Add flour and 1 teaspoon salt; beat 2 minutes more or till smooth. Pour the batter over the drippings in the pan(s).

● Bake the batter in a 400° oven about 35 to 40 minutes for roasting pan or about.30 to 35 minutes for round baking pans. Cut into squares or wedges to serve. Serve at once with roast. Makes 10 servings.

Rolled Flank Steak

Herbed Pot Roast Supreme

Sour cream and mushrooms add elegance to this seasoned pot roast.

2   slices bacon
1   2- to 3-pound beef chuck pot
     roast
1   10½-ounce can condensed
     beef broth
½   cup chopped onion
1   bay leaf
1   teaspoon Worcestershire
     sauce
½   teaspoon dried thyme,
     crushed
½   cup dairy sour cream
2   tablespoons all-purpose
     flour
1   4-ounce can mushroom
     stems and pieces, drained
2   tablespoons snipped parsley
     Hot cooked noodles

● In a Dutch oven cook the bacon till crisp. Drain, reserving the drippings. Crumble bacon; set aside.

● Trim excess fat from meat. Brown meat in reserved bacon drippings. Add the beef broth, chopped onion, bay leaf, Worcestershire sauce, thyme, ¼ teaspoon *salt,* and ⅛ teaspoon *pepper.* Cover and simmer for 1½ to 2 hours or till meat is tender. Transfer meat to a heated platter; keep warm.

● For sour cream sauce, skim fat from pan juices; discard bay leaf. Stir together the sour cream and flour. Stir about ¼ *cup* of the pan juices into the sour cream mixture; return all to pan. Cook and stir till thickened; *do not boil.* Stir in mushrooms, snipped parsley, and crumbled bacon. Serve sour cream sauce with roast and hot cooked noodles. Makes 8 to 12 servings.

Pot Roast and Gravy

1   3- to 4-pound beef chuck pot
       roast
2   tablespoons cooking oil
¾   cup water, wine, *or* beer
1   tablespoon Worcestershire
       sauce
1½   teaspoons dried basil,
       thyme, marjoram, *or*
       oregano, crushed
4   medium potatoes, peeled
       and quartered, *or* 16
       whole new potatoes
4   medium carrots, cut into
       1-inch pieces
4   stalks celery, bias-sliced
       into ½-inch pieces
2   medium onions, sliced and
       separated into rings
       Water, wine, *or* beer
½   cup cold water
¼   cup all-purpose flour
       Kitchen Bouquet (optional)

● Trim excess fat from the pot roast, leaving about ⅛ inch fat on the roast; discard. In an ovenproof Dutch oven brown the meat on both sides in the oil over medium heat (about 10 minutes total). Sprinkle with pepper. In a small bowl stir together the ¾ cup water, wine, or beer; Worcestershire sauce; basil, thyme, marjoram, or oregano; ½ teaspoon *salt;* and ⅛ teaspoon *pepper.* Pour over the roast. Cover; roast in a 325° oven for 1 hour.

● If using new potatoes, peel a strip from around the center of each potato. Place potatoes, carrots, celery, and onions around and on top of the pot roast. Cover and roast in a 325° oven about 1½ to 1¾ hours or till the roast and vegetables are tender. Transfer to a serving platter.

● For gravy, pour the juices from the Dutch oven into a measuring cup; spoon off fat. Add additional water, wine, or beer to the remaining juices, if necessary, to make *1½ cups* liquid. Return liquid to Dutch oven. In a screw-top jar shake together the ½ cup water and the flour. Stir into liquid in Dutch oven. Cook and stir over medium heat till thickened and bubbly. Cook and stir 1 minute more. If a darker gravy is desired, stir in a few drops of Kitchen Bouquet. Spoon some of the gravy over the vegetables and meat. Pass remaining gravy. Makes 8 servings.

Roasting Beef and Veal

Individual cuts of meat vary in size, shape, and tenderness. Because of these differences, use the roasting times only as a guide.

Cut	Approx. Weight (Pounds)	Internal Temperature on Removal from Oven	Approx. Cooking Time (Total Time)
Roast meat at constant oven temperature of 325° unless otherwise indicated.			
BEEF			
Rib Roast	4 to 6	140° (rare)	2 to 2½ hrs.
		160° (medium)	2½ to 3¼ hrs.
		170° (well-done)	2¾ to 4 hrs.
Rib Roast	6 to 8	140° (rare)	2½ to 3 hrs.
		160° (medium)	3 to 3½ hrs.
		170° (well-done)	3½ to 4¼ hrs.
Boneless Rib Roast	5 to 7	140° (rare)	2¾ to 3¾ hrs.
		160° (medium)	3¼ to 4¼ hrs.
		170° (well-done)	4 to 5½ hrs.
Boneless Round Rump Roast	4 to 6	150° to 170°	2 to 2½ hrs.
Round Tip Roast	3½ to 4	140° to 170°	2¼ to 2½ hrs.
Rib Eye Roast (Roast at 350°)	4 to 6	140° (rare)	1¼ to 1¾ hrs.
		160° (medium)	1½ to 2 hrs.
		170° (well-done)	1¾ to 2¼ hrs.
Tenderloin Roast (Roast at 425°)	4 to 6	140° (rare)	¾ to 1 hr.
Veal			
Leg Round Roast	5 to 8	170° (well-done)	2¾ to 3¼ hrs.
Loin Roast	4 to 6	170° (well-done)	2¼ to 3 hrs.
Boneless Shoulder Roast	4 to 6	170° (well-done)	3 to 4 hrs.

Roasting directions: Season the roast by sprinkling with a little salt and pepper. Insert a meat thermometer into the center of the roast so that the bulb reaches the thickest part of the lean meat. Make sure the bulb does not rest in fat or touch bone. Place roast, fat side up, on a rack in a shallow roasting pan. *Do not* cover, add water, or baste. Except as noted above, roast meat in 325° oven till the meat thermometer registers the desired internal temperature. To check doneness, push the thermometer into meat a little farther. If the temperature drops, continue cooking the meat to the desired temperature. Let meat stand about 15 minutes for easier carving. Remove string from rolled and tied roasts, and carve meat across the grain.

Horseradish- and Barley-Stuffed Rib Roast

⅓ cup quick-cooking barley
¼ cup sliced green onion
¼ cup prepared horseradish
2 cloves garlic, minced
¼ teaspoon salt
1 5- to 6-pound boneless beef
   rib roast

● Cook the barley according to package directions. Stir the green onion, horseradish, garlic, and salt into the cooked barley. Unroll the roast; spread evenly with the barley mixture. Reroll the roast and tie securely.

● Place the stuffed roast, fat side up, on a rack in a shallow roasting pan; sprinkle with a little salt and pepper. Insert meat thermometer. Roast in a 325° oven for 2¾ to 3 hours for medium-rare or till thermometer registers 145° (see chart, page 13). Let the roast stand about 15 minutes before carving. Remove the strings and carve. Makes 10 to 12 servings.

New England Boiled Dinner

1 3- to 4-pound corned beef
   brisket
10 small onions
4 medium potatoes, peeled
   and quartered
4 medium carrots, quartered
3 medium parsnips, peeled
   and sliced ½ inch thick
2 medium rutabagas, peeled
   and cut into 1-inch cubes
1 small head cabbage, cored
   and cut into wedges
Prepared horseradish
   (optional)
Prepared mustard (optional)
Assorted pickles (optional)

● Place the corned beef brisket in a 6- or 8-quart Dutch oven. Add enough *water* to cover the brisket. Bring water to boiling; reduce heat. Cover and simmer about 2 hours or till the meat is nearly tender.

● Add the onions, potatoes, carrots, parsnips, and rutabagas. Cover and simmer for 15 minutes. Add the cabbage wedges; cover and simmer 15 to 20 minutes more or till the cabbage is tender. Season to taste with salt and pepper.

● Serve the corned beef on a platter surrounded by vegetables. Serve with horseradish, mustard, and pickles, if desired. Pass some of the pan juices. Makes 8 to 10 servings.

Stroganoff-Style Round Steak

To ensure a smooth sauce, thoroughly combine the flour and sour cream before adding the mixture to the meat juices.

1 ¾-pound beef round steak, cut ¾ inch thick
4 teaspoons all-purpose flour
½ teaspoon salt
⅛ teaspoon pepper
1 tablespoon cooking oil
¾ cup water
1 small onion, sliced
1 teaspoon instant beef bouillon granules
¼ teaspoon dried oregano *or* basil, crushed
4 teaspoons all-purpose flour
½ cup dairy sour cream *or* plain yogurt
6 cups water
¼ teaspoon salt
4 ounces noodles
Snipped parsley (optional)

● Trim fat from the meat; remove any bone. Cut into four serving-size pieces. In a custard cup combine 4 teaspoons flour, ½ teaspoon salt, and pepper. Sprinkle about *half* of the flour mixture over one side of the meat pieces. Use a meat mallet to pound the meat from the center to the outside edges. Turn meat over; sprinkle with the remaining flour mixture and pound with a meat mallet.

● In a heavy 10-inch skillet heat the oil. Add the meat; brown quickly on both sides. Remove from heat. Stir in the water, onion, bouillon granules, and oregano or basil. Cover; cook over low heat about 1¼ hours or till meat is tender.

● For sauce, remove the meat from the skillet; cover with foil. Pour meat juices from the skillet into a glass measure. Use a spoon to skim off fat. Measure ¾ cup juices (if necessary, add *water* to equal ¾ *cup* liquid). Return juice mixture to skillet. Stir 4 teaspoons flour into the sour cream or yogurt. Stir into the juice mixture. Cook and stir over medium heat till thickened and bubbly. Cook and stir 1 minute more.

● Meanwhile, in a Dutch oven bring the water and the ¼ teaspoon salt to a boil. Add the noodles, a few at a time, stirring constantly. Cook the noodles in boiling salted water for 8 to 10 minutes or till tender. Drain. Top noodles with meat and sauce. If desired, sprinkle with parsley. Makes 4 servings.

Steak with Onion-Wine Sauce

6 beef tenderloin steaks, cut 1 inch thick (1¾ pounds total)
1 tablespoon butter *or* margarine
1 tablespoon olive oil
¼ cup sliced green onion
½ cup dry red wine
2 tablespoons snipped parsley
½ teaspoon salt
Dash pepper
2 tablespoons butter *or* margarine

● In a 10-inch skillet cook the steaks in the 1 tablespoon butter and the olive oil over medium-high heat to desired doneness, turning once. (Allow 9 to 10 minutes total cooking time for rare, 11 to 12 minutes for medium.) Season the steaks with a little salt and pepper. Transfer the meat to a serving platter; keep meat warm while preparing the sauce.

● For sauce, in the same skillet cook the sliced green onion in drippings till tender but not brown. Add the wine, parsley, ½ teaspoon salt, and dash pepper; stir to loosen crusty bits from bottom of pan. Heat and stir till sauce is bubbly. Stir in 2 tablespoons butter just till melted. Serve immediately over hot steaks. Makes 6 servings.

Almond-Sauced Steak for Two

1   ¾-pound beef sirloin,
      porterhouse, *or* T-bone
      steak, cut 1½ inches thick
1   cup sliced fresh mushrooms
2   tablespoons snipped chives
2   tablespoons toasted slivered
      almonds
2   tablespoons butter
⅓   cup dry white wine
¼   teaspoon salt
⅛   teaspoon dried fines herbes,
      crushed

● Place steak on an unheated rack of a broiler pan. Broil 4 inches from heat for 8 minutes; turn and broil 6 to 8 minutes more for rare or to desired doneness (see chart, page 21).
● Meanwhile, in a small skillet cook the sliced mushrooms, snipped chives, and toasted slivered almonds in butter till the mushrooms and chives are tender. Stir in the dry white wine, salt, and fines herbes; heat through, but *do not boil*. Serve over steak. Makes 2 servings.

Boeuf en Daube

2   slices bacon, cut up
2   to 2½ pounds beef stew
      meat, cut into 1-inch
      cubes
2   cups dry red wine
½   cup water
1   medium onion, chopped
      (½ cup)
2   cloves garlic, minced
1   tablespoon vinegar
½   teaspoon salt
½   teaspoon instant beef
      bouillon granules
½   teaspoon dried rosemary,
      crushed
½   teaspoon dried thyme,
      crushed
½   teaspoon finely shredded
      orange peel
¼   teaspoon pepper
6   carrots, bias-sliced into
      1-inch pieces
3   medium onions, quartered
1   cup pitted ripe olives
2   tablespoons cornstarch
2   tablespoons cold water
      Snipped parsley (optional)

● In a Dutch oven cook bacon till crisp. Add the meat cubes; brown the meat in the bacon drippings. Stir in the red wine, the ½ cup water, the chopped onion, garlic, vinegar, salt, beef bouillon granules, rosemary, thyme, orange peel, and pepper. Bring to boiling.
● Reduce heat; cover and simmer for 1 hour. Stir in carrots, quartered onions, and olives. Simmer, covered, for 30 to 40 minutes or till vegetables are tender.
● Stir together the cornstarch and the 2 tablespoons cold water; stir into the meat mixture. Cook and stir till thickened and bubbly. Cook and stir 2 minutes more. Turn into a serving bowl. Top with snipped parsley, if desired. Makes 8 servings.

Boeuf en Daube

Veal Piccata

1 **pound veal leg round** *or* **veal leg sirloin steak**
3 **tablespoons butter**
1 **cup sliced fresh mushrooms**
3 **tablespoons lemon juice**
¼ **teaspoon dried basil, crushed**
¼ **teaspoon salt**
  Dash pepper
2 **tablespoons snipped parsley**

● With a meat mallet, pound the veal to ¼-inch thickness. Cut the veal into four pieces. In a 10-inch skillet cook *half* of the veal in hot butter over medium-high heat for 1 minute on each side. Transfer the meat to a heated platter; keep meat warm. Add a little more butter to the skillet, if necessary; cook the remaining half of the veal. Transfer to the platter; keep the cooked meat warm while preparing the sauce.

● For sauce, to the butter remaining in the skillet add the sliced mushrooms, lemon juice, basil, salt, and pepper. Cover; cook the mixture for 5 minutes or till the mushrooms are tender. Stir in the snipped parsley. Spoon the sauce over the veal. Serve at once. Makes 4 servings.

Garden Steak Rolls

1½ **pounds boneless beef round steak**
3 **slices bacon, halved crosswise**
1 **9-ounce package frozen whole green beans, thawed,** *or* **2 cups fresh green beans**
3 **small carrots, cut into julienne strips**
  Salt
  Pepper
  Garlic powder
1 **10¼-ounce can beef gravy**

● Cut steak into six portions; pound to ¼-inch thickness. In a 10-inch skillet cook bacon just till done; drain on paper towels, reserving drippings in skillet.

● Place a piece of bacon and several green beans and carrots on each meat portion. Sprinkle with salt, pepper, and garlic powder. Roll up meat jelly-roll style. Secure with wooden picks.

● Brown meat on all sides in hot drippings; drain off fat. Add gravy; cover and simmer for 40 minutes. Uncover; cook 10 to 15 minutes more or till gravy is thickened and meat is tender. Remove picks from meat before serving. Makes 6 servings.

Fruited Veal Marsala

1 pound boneless veal round
 steak, cut ¼ inch thick
1 tablespoon lemon juice
½ teaspoon salt
⅛ teaspoon pepper
¼ cup all-purpose flour
3 tablespoons butter *or*
 margarine
⅓ cup orange juice
⅓ cup dry marsala
2 tablespoons water
¼ teaspoon instant chicken
 bouillon granules
1 small bay leaf
3 firm medium bananas,
 halved lengthwise and
 crosswise
¼ cup slivered almonds,
 toasted

● Cut the veal into six serving-size pieces; pound each to ⅛-inch thickness. Sprinkle with the lemon juice, salt, and pepper; coat with flour. In a skillet brown the meat, half at a time, in the butter or margarine for 1 minute on each side. Transfer the meat to a serving platter; keep meat warm.

● Add the orange juice, marsala, water, bouillon, and bay leaf to the skillet. Simmer, uncovered, for 3 minutes. Add the banana pieces; cook for 2 minutes on each side.

● Remove the bay leaf; discard. Arrange the banana pieces atop the meat; pour the pan juices over all. Top with the toasted slivered almonds. Makes 6 servings.

Burgundy Beef Shanks with Wild Rice

¼ cup all-purpose flour
1 teaspoon salt
¼ teaspoon pepper
2 pounds beef shank
 crosscuts
2 tablespoons cooking oil
1 leek *or* medium onion, sliced
1 clove garlic, minced
1½ cups Burgundy *or* dry
 white wine
4 parsley sprigs
1 bay leaf, crumbled
1 6-ounce package long
 grain and wild rice mix
2 10-ounce packages frozen
 broccoli spears, thawed,
 or 1 pound fresh broccoli
 spears

● Stir together the flour, salt, and pepper. Coat the beef with the flour mixture. In a Dutch oven brown the meat, half at a time, in hot oil. Transfer the browned meat to paper towels, reserving drippings in pan.

● Cook the sliced leek or onion and minced garlic in the reserved drippings till tender but not brown; drain off the fat. Return the meat to the pan. Stir in the Burgundy or dry white wine, parsley, and bay leaf.

● Bring to boiling; reduce heat. Cover; simmer for 30 minutes. Stir in 1½ cups *water* and the rice mix. Cover and cook 45 minutes more. Add the broccoli spears; cover and cook 15 minutes more. Makes 6 servings.

Oven method: Cook the meat, leek, and garlic as directed; add the Burgundy, parsley, and bay leaf. Bake, covered, in a 350° oven for 1 hour. Stir in 1½ cups *water* and the rice mix. Cover and bake 15 minutes more. Add the broccoli; cover and bake the mixture 45 minutes more.

Marinated Steak

Scoring the meat shortens the meat fibers, making them more tender. Use a sharp knife to make long shallow cuts about ⅛ to ¼ inch deep.

1   1- to 1½-pound beef flank
       steak
⅓   cup soy sauce
2   tablespoons water
2   tablespoons dry sherry
1   tablespoon cooking oil
2   cloves garlic, minced
½   teaspoon sugar
½   teaspoon ground ginger

● With a sharp knife score the steak at 1-inch intervals on both sides in a diamond pattern. Place the steak in a plastic bag; set it in a shallow baking dish.

● For the marinade, stir together the soy sauce, water, sherry, cooking oil, garlic, sugar, and ginger. Pour the marinade over the steak; close the bag. Chill in the refrigerator for 6 to 24 hours, turning the bag occasionally to distribute the marinade evenly over the meat.

● Remove the steak from the bag; drain well. Place the steak on an unheated rack of a broiler pan. Broil 3 inches from the heat to desired doneness, turning once. (Allow 8 to 10 minutes total time for medium-rare doneness.)

● To serve, slice the meat diagonally across the grain into very thin slices. Spoon the juices from the broiler pan over the meat. Makes 4 to 6 servings.

Lime Steak for Two

8   ounces beef cubed steak
      Salt
      Pepper
1   tablespoon cooking oil
½   cup sliced fresh
       mushrooms
1   tablespoon butter *or*
       margarine
2   tablespoons water
1   tablespoon lime juice
      Lime slices (optional)

● Cut the steak into two serving-size portions. Sprinkle each piece of meat with salt and pepper.

● In a small skillet cook the steaks over medium heat in hot cooking oil about 1 minute on each side or till the meat is brown on both sides; cook for 1 minute more. Remove the steaks, reserving the drippings in the skillet. Set the steaks aside.

● To the reserved drippings in the skillet add the sliced mushrooms and butter or margarine; cook about 5 minutes or till the mushrooms are tender but not brown. Stir in the water and lime juice. Bring the mixture to boiling.

● Return the steaks to the skillet; cook for 1 minute more or till the steaks are heated through. Garnish the meat with lime slices, if desired. Makes 2 servings.

Steak Piccata: Prepare Lime Steak for Two as directed above, *except* substitute 1 tablespoon *lemon juice* and *lemon slices* for the lime juice and lime slices.

Broiling Beef Steaks

Thickness	1 inch	1½ inches	2 inches
	(approximate total time in minutes)		
Rare	8 to 10	14 to 16	20 to 25
Medium	12 to 14	18 to 20	30 to 35
Well-Done	18 to 20	25 to 30	40 to 45

To test a broiled or grilled beef steak for doneness, slit the center of the steak and note the inside color: red–rare; pink–medium; gray–well-done.

Choose a beef porterhouse, T-bone, top loin, sirloin, or tenderloin steak cut 1 to 2 inches thick. Without cutting into the meat, slash the fat edge at 1-inch intervals. Place the steak on the unheated rack in a broiler pan.

Broil 1- to 1½-inch-thick steaks so surface of meat is 3 inches from heat. Broil 2-inch cuts 4 to 5 inches from heat. (Check range instruction booklet.) Broil on one side for about half of the time indicated in chart for desired doneness. Season with a little salt and pepper, if desired. Turn with tongs and broil till desired doneness. Season again.

Grilling Beef Steaks Outdoors

Thickness	1 inch		1½ inches
Temperature of Coals	Medium-hot	Medium	Medium-hot
	(approximate total time in minutes)		
Open Grill Rare	12 to 18	20 to 25	18 to 20
Medium	15 to 20	25 to 30	20 to 25
Covered Grill Rare	8 to 10	15 to 18	10 to 15
Medium	10 to 15	18 to 22	15 to 18

Choose beef porterhouse, T-bone, or sirloin steaks. Slash the fat edge at 1-inch intervals to keep steaks flat on grill. To estimate temperature of coals, hold hand, palm side down, about 4 inches above coals. Count seconds "one thousand one, one thousand two," and so on. When you can hold your hand comfortably over the coals for only 2 to 3 seconds, they have a temperature of *medium-hot;* 3 to 4 seconds indicate *medium.* Grill steaks for about half of the time indicated in the chart for desired doneness. Flip steaks using tongs and pancake turner (piercing with fork wastes good meat juices); grill till steaks are desired doneness.

Veal Chops with Lemon Sauce for Two

2 veal loin chops, cut
   ½ inch thick (½ pound)
1 2-ounce can mushroom
   stems and pieces
2 teaspoons butter *or*
   margarine
⅓ cup skim milk
1½ teaspoons cornstarch
2 teaspoons lemon juice
¼ teaspoon salt
   Dash pepper
   Dash dried tarragon,
   crushed

● Place the chops on an unheated rack of a broiler pan. Broil 3 to 4 inches from the heat for 5 minutes. Turn chops; sprinkle with salt and pepper. Broil about 5 minutes more or till done.
● Meanwhile, prepare the sauce. In a small saucepan combine the *undrained* mushrooms and butter or margarine. Cook and stir over low heat till the butter is melted.
● In a screw-top jar combine the milk and cornstarch; shake well. Add to mushroom-butter mixture in the saucepan. Cook and stir over medium heat till thickened and bubbly. Remove from heat; stir in the lemon juice, salt, pepper, and tarragon. Spoon the sauce over the chops. Makes 2 servings.

Individual Beef Wellingtons

When you are expecting guests, keep last-minute preparations simple by making this elegant entrée the night before.

4 beef tenderloin steaks *or*
   beef eye round steaks, cut
   1 inch thick
   Cooking oil
4 frozen patty shells, thawed
¼ cup canned liver spread
1 beaten egg
½ cup cold water
1½ teaspoons cornstarch
1 teaspoon instant beef
   bouillon granules
¼ teaspoon dried basil,
   crushed
2 tablespoons dry red wine

● Brush steaks with cooking oil; sprinkle with a little salt and pepper. In a hot skillet quickly brown steaks for 2 minutes on each side. Cool at least 15 minutes.
● Roll each thawed patty shell into an 8-inch circle. Spread the liver over the pastry circles to within 1 inch of the edge. Center *one* steak atop *each* pastry circle. Wrap meat in pastry; brush the edge of the pastry with a little beaten egg. Press the edges of the pastry to seal. Place the pastry-wrapped meat, seam side down, in a greased shallow baking pan. Use a sharp knife to make a small slash in the top of each. Cover and chill up to 24 hours. Cover and chill the remaining beaten egg.
● To bake, brush the remaining egg over the pastry. Bake in a 425° oven about 20 minutes for medium doneness. Meanwhile, prepare sauce. In a small saucepan combine water, cornstarch, bouillon granules, and basil. Cook and stir till thickened and bubbly. Cook and stir 2 minutes more. Stir in the red wine. Serve the sauce over the beef Wellingtons. Makes 4 servings.

Sweet and Spicy Ribs

3 pounds beef or pork
　　spareribs
2 tablespoons cooking oil *or*
　　shortening
1½ cups water
1 large onion, chopped (1 cup)
1 medium apple, cored and
　　sliced into rings
2 cloves garlic, minced
2 tablespoons sugar
1½ teaspoons instant beef
　　bouillon granules
1 teaspoon salt
¼ teaspoon pepper
⅛ teaspoon ground cloves
2 tablespoons cold water
2 tablespoons cornstarch
¼ teaspoon Kitchen Bouquet
　　(optional)

● Cut meat into two- or three-rib portions. In a large heavy oven-proof skillet or 4-quart Dutch oven, brown the ribs in hot oil or shortening, a few pieces at a time, for 3 to 4 minutes or till browned on both sides. Drain off excess fat. Return all ribs to the skillet or Dutch oven.

● Add the 1½ cups water, the chopped onion, apple rings, garlic, sugar, beef bouillon granules, salt, pepper, and cloves. Cover and bake in a 350° oven for 2 hours for beef ribs (or 1½ hours for pork ribs) or till meat is tender. Remove ribs to a heated serving platter; keep ribs warm.

● To make gravy, pour pan juices into a measuring cup. Skim off the fat. Add water, if necessary, to make *2 cups* liquid. Return liquid to the pan. Combine the 2 tablespoons cold water and the cornstarch; stir into the pan juices. Cook and stir till thickened and bubbly. Add Kitchen Bouquet, if desired. Serve the gravy with ribs. Makes 4 to 6 servings.

Scandinavian Short Ribs for Two

¼ cup chopped onion
1 tablespoon butter *or*
　　margarine
1 5½-ounce can apple
　　cider *or* apple juice
2 teaspoons catsup
⅛ teaspoon salt
⅛ teaspoon dried basil,
　　crushed
Dash ground allspice
Dash ground cloves
4 beef short ribs, cut into
　　serving-size pieces
　　(about 1 pound)
1 tablespoon cold water
2 teaspoons cornstarch
2 teaspoons pickle relish
　　(optional)

● In a medium saucepan cook the onion in butter or margarine till tender but not brown. Stir in the apple cider or juice, catsup, salt, basil, allspice, and cloves. Trim fat from ribs; add the ribs to the saucepan. Bring to boiling; reduce heat. Cover; simmer for 1¼ to 1½ hours or till meat is tender. Transfer ribs to a serving platter, reserving cooking liquid; keep warm.

● For the sauce, skim fat from the cooking liquid. Measure cooking liquid; add water, if necessary, to make ⅔ cup. Stir together the 1 tablespoon water and the cornstarch; stir into cooking liquid. Cook and stir till the mixture is thickened and bubbly. Cook and stir 2 minutes more. Stir in the pickle relish, if desired. Spoon some of the sauce over the ribs. Pass the remaining sauce. Makes 2 servings.

Quick Crescent Quiche

Quick Crescent Quiche

1 package (8) refrigerated
   crescent rolls
1 cup chopped cooked beef
1 4-ounce can sliced
   mushrooms, drained
1 cup shredded Swiss cheese
   (4 ounces)
2 beaten eggs
1 5⅓-ounce can (⅔ cup)
   evaporated milk
2 teaspoons diced dried
   bell pepper
¼ teaspoon dried thyme,
   crushed
   Bottled hot pepper sauce
¼ cup slivered almonds
1 tablespoon snipped
   parsley

● For the crust, separate the crescent rolls into eight triangles. In an ungreased 9-inch pie plate or quiche dish, arrange the dough triangles with their points toward the center of the dish. Press the dough over the bottom and sides of the dish, pinching the edges together to seal.

● Sprinkle the cooked beef and mushrooms over the crust. Sprinkle the shredded Swiss cheese over all. Combine the eggs, evaporated milk, dried bell pepper, thyme, and *few dashes* hot pepper sauce; pour over the cheese. Top with slivered almonds and snipped parsley. Cover the crust edges with foil to prevent overbrowning. Bake in a 350° oven about 30 minutes or till almost set. Makes 6 servings.

Mexican Beef Salad

½ teaspoon instant meat
   tenderizer
1 pound boneless beef round
   steak
2 tablespoons cooking oil
1 onion
1 green pepper
¼ cup sliced pitted ripe olives
¼ cup sliced green olives
1 16-ounce can yellow
   hominy, drained
2 tablespoons cooking oil
½ teaspoon chili powder
¼ teaspoon ground cumin
¼ teaspoon dried oregano,
   crushed
⅛ teaspoon crushed red
   pepper
⅛ teaspoon garlic powder
3 tablespoons vinegar
½ cup halved cherry tomatoes
1 cup shredded Monterey
   Jack cheese (4 ounces)
6 cups torn lettuce

● Sprinkle the meat tenderizer over the beef round steak. With a fork pierce the meat. Slice the meat across the grain into very thin bite-size strips.

● In a skillet brown the meat in 2 tablespoons cooking oil. With a slotted spoon transfer the browned meat to a bowl. Slice the onion and green pepper into rings; add to meat in the bowl. Top with ripe olives, green olives, and hominy.

● For the salad dressing, to the skillet drippings add 2 tablespoons cooking oil. Stir in the chili powder, ground cumin, oregano, red pepper, garlic powder, and ½ teaspoon *salt*. Cook and stir till heated through; remove from heat. Stir in the vinegar. Pour over the meat mixture. Cover; chill 3 hours.

● To serve, toss the meat-dressing mixture with the halved cherry tomatoes and the Monterey Jack cheese. Line a large bowl with *lettuce leaves.* Add the torn lettuce and meat mixture; toss to coat. Makes 6 to 8 servings.

Beef Paprika

1 pound beef stew meat, cut into 1-inch cubes
1 large onion, chopped (1 cup)
3 tablespoons cooking oil
1 16-ounce can tomatoes, cut up
1 cup water
1 tablespoon paprika
1 tablespoon dried parsley flakes
2 teaspoons instant beef bouillon granules
½ teaspoon dried thyme, crushed
¼ teaspoon salt
⅛ teaspoon minced dried garlic
1 bay leaf
2 tablespoons cold water
1 tablespoon all-purpose flour
Hot cooked noodles

● In a 10-inch ovenproof skillet cook the meat and chopped onion in hot cooking oil till the meat is brown and the onion is tender. Drain off fat. Stir in the *undrained* tomatoes, 1 cup water, paprika, parsley flakes, beef bouillon granules, thyme, salt, dried garlic, and bay leaf. Bring the mixture to boiling. Remove from heat; cover.

● Bake the mixture, covered, in a 350° oven about 1½ hours or till the meat is tender. Skim off the fat. Stir together the 2 tablespoons water and flour. Stir into the mixture in the skillet. Cook and stir till thickened and bubbly. Cook and stir 1 minute more. Remove the bay leaf. Serve the meat mixture over hot cooked noodles. Makes 4 servings.

Making Beef Jerky

To make beef jerky, remove and discard all the fat from 1 pound of *beef top round steak*, then freeze the steak until it's icy. Cut the partially frozen meat into very thin strips, cutting across the grain for crisp jerky, or with the grain for chewy jerky.

Place some of the meat strips in a bowl or crock to make a ½-inch-thick layer. Sprinkle the meat with *salt, pepper,* and *liquid smoke.* Repeat layers until all of the meat is used.

Weight the meat with a plate or heavy object; cover and chill in the refrigerator overnight. Drain the meat, then pat it dry with paper towels. Arrange the meat on a rack in a shallow baking pan. Bake in a 250° oven for 3½ to 4 hours or to desired dryness. Cool.

Store the jerky in airtight plastic bags or in a jar with a tight-fitting lid in the refrigerator or at cool room temperature. This recipe makes about ½ pound of beef jerky.

Veal in Cream Sauce

½ pound boneless veal *or* pork
1 tablespoon butter *or* margarine
1 medium carrot, sliced
1 cup sliced fresh mushrooms
¼ cup sliced green onion
½ cup chicken broth
¼ teaspoon salt
  Dash pepper
½ cup light cream
1 tablespoon all-purpose flour
  Hot cooked noodles

● Partially freeze the veal or pork; thinly slice into julienne strips. In a wok or large skillet melt butter or margarine over medium-high heat. Add the sliced veal or pork; stir-fry for 1 minute. Remove from wok.

● Add the sliced carrot, mushrooms, and green onion; stir-fry for 3 minutes. Add the chicken broth, salt, and pepper; cover and cook about 5 minutes or till the carrots are done.

● Stir the light cream into the flour; stir into the vegetable mixture. Cook and stir till thickened and bubbly. Cook and stir 1 minute more. Return the meat to the wok or skillet; heat through. Serve over hot cooked noodles. Garnish with green onion brushes, if desired. Makes 2 or 3 servings.

Veal Stew

If you use beef stew meat instead of veal, simmer the beef with the juice-lentil mixture for 30 minutes before adding the vegetables.

¾ pound veal *or* beef stew meat, cut into ¾-inch cubes
1 large onion, chopped (1 cup)
1 clove garlic, minced
1 tablespoon cooking oil
2 12-ounce cans vegetable juice cocktail
¼ cup dry lentils
1 bay leaf
2 teaspoons lemon juice
½ teaspoon dried basil, crushed
1 large stalk celery, sliced
1 parsnip, sliced
1 cup sliced fresh mushrooms
1 cup coarsely chopped cabbage
2 small potatoes, cut into 1-inch chunks

● In a Dutch oven or a large saucepan cook the meat, onion, and garlic in hot oil till the meat is brown and the onion is tender. Drain off the fat. Add the vegetable juice cocktail, lentils, bay leaf, lemon juice, and basil. Bring to boiling.

● Add the sliced celery, parsnip, mushrooms, chopped cabbage, and cut-up potatoes. Reduce heat. Cover and simmer over low heat for 50 to 60 minutes or till the vegetables are tender. Remove the bay leaf before serving. Makes 6 servings.

Old-Fashioned Fresh Vegetable-Beef Soup

3 pounds beef shank
   crosscuts
½ teaspoon dried oregano,
   crushed
¼ teaspoon dried marjoram,
   crushed
5 whole black peppercorns
2 bay leaves
4 fresh ears of corn *or*
   1 10-ounce package
   frozen whole kernel corn
3 tomatoes, peeled and cut up
2 medium potatoes, peeled
   and cubed (2 cups)
1 cup fresh cut green beans *or*
   ½ of a 9-ounce package
   frozen cut green beans
1 cup sliced carrots
2 stalks celery, sliced (1 cup)
½ cup chopped onion

● In a large kettle or Dutch oven combine the beef shank crosscuts, 8 cups *water,* 4 teaspoons *salt,* oregano, marjoram, peppercorns, and bay leaves. Bring the mixture to boiling. Reduce heat; cover and simmer about 2 hours.
● Remove the beef. When cool enough to handle, cut the meat from the bones; chop the meat. Strain the broth; skim off the fat. Return the broth to the kettle. Cut fresh corn from the cobs.
● Add the chopped meat, the fresh or frozen corn, tomatoes, potatoes, fresh or frozen green beans, carrots, celery, and onion to the kettle or Dutch oven. Cover and simmer about 1 hour or till the vegetables are tender. Season to taste with salt and pepper. Makes 10 to 12 servings.

Texas-Style Chili

2½ pounds beef round steak,
   cut into ½-inch cubes
3 tablespoons cooking oil
½ cup chopped onion
1 clove garlic, minced
1 10½-ounce can condensed
   beef broth
2 teaspoons sugar
2 teaspoons dried oregano,
   crushed
2 teaspoons cumin seed,
   crushed
½ to ¾ teaspoon ground red
   pepper
½ teaspoon paprika
2 bay leaves
1 4-ounce can chopped green
   chili peppers
2 tablespoons cornmeal
   Hot cooked rice
   Hot cooked pinto beans

● In a large saucepan or Dutch oven brown *half* of the beef cubes in hot oil; remove meat and set aside. Add remaining meat, onion, and garlic; cook till meat is brown. Return all meat to saucepan. Stir in beef broth, 1 soup can (1⅓ cups) *water,* sugar, oregano, cumin seed, ground red pepper, paprika, and bay leaves. Bring to boiling; reduce heat. Simmer, uncovered, about 1½ hours or till meat is tender.
● Stir in chopped green chili peppers and cornmeal. Simmer 20 minutes more, stirring occasionally. Remove bay leaves. Serve with hot cooked rice and beans. Makes 6 to 8 servings.

Roasts from the Shoulder

The pork shoulder includes the Boston shoulder from the upper area and the arm picnic or arm shoulder from the lower area.

Shoulder Arm Roast A square-shaped roast that is cut from the upper portion of the Arm Picnic. Contains the round arm bone. *Roast.*

Shoulder Arm Picnic The round arm bone identifies this roast from the lower shoulder area. It is less tender than the upper Blade Boston Roast. May be sold boned, rolled, and tied. Also called fresh picnic. *Roast.* When cured and smoked, it is labeled **Smoked Arm Picnic** or simply smoked picnic. This is often confused with ham, and is prepared similarly. May be labeled "fully cooked" or "cook-before-eating." *Bake or cook in liquid.*

Shoulder Blade Boston Roast A square-shaped roast with identifying blade bone from the upper shoulder. Sometimes called Boston butt. Also sold with bone removed, rolled, and tied. *Roast.* When cured and smoked, it is labeled **Smoked Pork Shoulder Roll.** *Bake or cook in liquid.*

Ribs

Include the meaty **Country-Style Ribs,** the **Loin Back Ribs,** and the mostly bone **Spareribs.** *Roast, braise, cook in liquid,* or *broil slowly (often broiled on outdoor grill).*

Since the pork carcass is smaller than the beef, it is halved but not quartered. Wholesale cuts include the shoulder, the loin, the leg (ham), and the side, as shown. The loin is the most tender area with tenderness decreasing as cuts are made closer to the shoulder and to the leg.

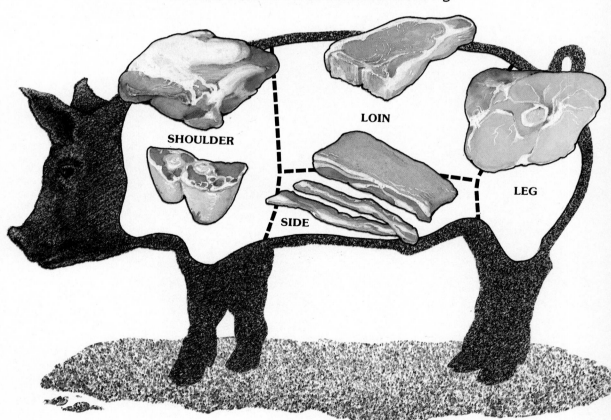

SHOULDER

LOIN

LEG

SIDE

Steaks from the Shoulder

Shoulder Arm Steak Cut from the Arm Picnic. Contains the identifying round arm bone. *Braise or panfry.*

Shoulder Blade Steak Cut from the Blade Boston Roast. Contains blade bone. *Braise, broil, panbroil, or panfry.*

Cubed Steak Any boneless piece of pork which has been put through a tenderizing machine. *Braise, broil, panbroil, or panfry.*

Roasts from the Loin

Cuts from the loin are the most tender and usually the most expensive of all pork cuts.

Center Loin Roast Cut between Loin Blade Roast and Sirloin Roast. Includes a portion of the tenderloin. May be smoked. With tenderloin removed, it is a **Loin Center Rib Roast.** Two rib roasts tied together make a **Crown Roast.** *Roast.*

Boneless Top Loin Roast Flat-shaped loin eye muscle. May have two roasts tied, flat sides together, in a roll shape. *Roast.* Becomes **Canadian-Style Bacon** when shaped into compact roll, then cured and smoked. *Bake, broil, panbroil, or panfry.*

Sirloin Roast Cut from the loin section nearest the leg. Usually 5 to 7 inches in length. Contains the backbone and hip bone. *Roast.*

Loin Blade Roast Includes the first 5 to 7 rib bones. May have the blade bone removed. *Roast.*

Pork Tenderloin Small tapering muscle that extends through part of the loin. Usually weighs 1 pound or less. Also comes cured and smoked. *Roast, braise, or broil.*

Chops from the Loin
Sliced from loin roasts.

Sirloin Chop Cut from the loin section nearest the leg. Contains section of backbone and/or hip bone. May be smoked. Also called sirloin steak. *Braise, broil, panbroil, or panfry.*

Loin Blade Chop Cut from the first 5 to 7 ribs. May have the blade bone removed. *Braise, broil, panbroil, or panfry.*

Loin Rib Chop Tender rib eye muscle. May be smoked, boneless, and/or butterflied. When cut thicker, with pocket, it is known as **Loin Rib Chop for Stuffing.** *Braise, broil, panbroil, or panfry.*

Loin Chop Cut between Loin Rib Chop and Sirloin Chop. Includes a portion of tenderloin as well as the loin eye muscle. *Braise, broil, panbroil, or panfry.*

Sirloin Cutlet Boneless lean piece from the wedge-shaped area above the hip bone. Also called pork cutlet. *Braise, broil, panbroil, or panfry.*

Top Loin Chop From center loin section. Tenderloin removed; chine bone chipped. May be boneless and/or butterflied. *Braise, broil, panbroil, or panfry.*

Cuts from the Side and Other Areas

Pork Cubes for Kabobs Cut from the shoulder or leg (smoked ham). *Broil, braise, panfry, or roast.*

Pork Jowl Square piece in front of shoulder. Often smoked; may be sliced. *Broil, panbroil, panfry, or cook in liquid.*

Pork Hock Cut from shank (lower) end of arm or leg (ham). Mostly bone and cartilage with little meat. May be fresh, cured and smoked, or pickled. *Braise or cook in liquid.*

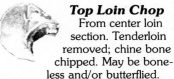

Fresh Side Pork Whole piece removed from side. May be sliced. Called salt pork when salt is rubbed on pieces. *Roast, broil, panbroil, panfry, or cook in liquid.* Cured and smoked to make **Slab Bacon**; also may be sliced. *Bake, broil, panbroil, or panfry.*

Pigs Feet May be fresh, smoked, or pickled. *Cook in liquid or braise.*

Ham

According to USDA standards, all meat labeled "ham" must come from the hind leg of a pig. It may be fresh, but is usually cured and smoked. Curing may be done by simply rubbing salt over the surface and storing in a cool place (dry salt cure). Or a salt solution may be pumped into the meat, left for a certain time, then rinsed away (brine cure). The ham is then cooked and, sometimes, smoked. All may be fully-cooked or require cooking before eating (see Ham Terminology below for cooking information).

Whole Ham Pear-shaped cut containing leg and shank bones. Usually weighs 10 to 18 pounds. *Bake.*

Center Slice Nearly round, meaty cut from center of whole ham. Contains small round leg bone, which may be removed. *Bake, broil, panbroil, or panfry.*

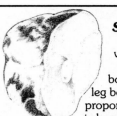

Shank Half Lower half of whole ham that includes shank bone and part of leg bone. Has lower proportion of meat to bone than rump half.

Rump Half Upper half of whole ham. Has more meat to bone than shank half. Called **Rump Portion** when center slice is removed.

Country-Style Ham

Distinctively-flavored ham that is dry cured. Usually saltier and firmer than smoked hams. Many types; must be processed in Smithfield, Va. to be labeled a Smithfield ham.

Follow label directions (usually must be scrubbed, soaked, and simmered before baking).

Boneless Ham

All of the bones and most of the interior and exterior fat are removed. Remaining lean meat is then shaped inside a casing or placed into a can and processed. A whole ham averages 7 to 10 pounds, but it is usually cut into halves, quarters, or pieces. Also referred to as a rolled, shaped, formed, or sectioned and formed ham. Usually fully-cooked; some require cooking before eating.

Partially Boned Ham

One or two of the three bones (shank, aitch, leg) in a whole ham are removed. Called a **Shankless Ham** when the shank bone is removed. Called a **Semi-Boneless Ham** when both the shank and aitch bones are removed, leaving only the round leg bone. Usually cut into two smaller pieces. All may be fully-cooked or require cooking before eating.

Canned Ham

Usually consists of boneless cured ham pieces that are placed in a can, then vacuum sealed and fully-cooked. A small amount of dry gelatin is added before sealing to absorb the natural ham juices while the ham cooks. Traditional pear-shaped canned hams range in weight from 1½ to 10 pounds. All canned hams are ready-to-eat. Most are labeled "perishable—keep refrigerated." Some may be shelf stable. Check the label.

Ham Terminology
Cured and Smoked
Describes the curing and smoking processes. May need additional baking to finish cooking and develop flavors. Should be refrigerated.
Fully Cooked Cured and smoked pork products which are completely cooked. Ready-to-eat but may be heated. Refrigerate.
Cook Before Eating
Indicates that the ham was not completely cooked during the smoking process. To serve, bake to an internal temperature of 160°.
Water Added Hams which retained water during the curing process so that they weigh more than they did before processing. Added moisture cannot exceed 10% of the weight of the fresh ham.

Apple-Stuffed Rib Roast

1 **4-pound pork loin center rib roast, backbone loosened**
Salt
Pepper
1 **20-ounce can sliced apples**
1 **pound ground pork**
9 **slices dry raisin bread, cut into ½-inch cubes**
1 **teaspoon ground cinnamon**
¾ **teaspoon salt**
½ **teaspoon ground cardamom**
¼ **teaspoon ground allspice**
Dash pepper
Fresh sage (optional)

● Place roast rib side down. Cut pockets in roast from meaty side between rib bones. Season with salt and pepper. Drain apples, reserving juice. Finely chop apples and set aside. Add water to reserved juice to make 1 cup liquid; set aside.
● For stuffing, in a skillet cook ground pork till no longer pink; drain off fat. Stir in the apples, bread cubes, cinnamon, the ¾ teaspoon salt, cardamom, allspice, and dash pepper. Add reserved apple liquid; toss to moisten. Spoon about ½ cup stuffing into each pocket of roast. (Spoon remaining stuffing into a 1-quart casserole; cover and refrigerate.)
● Place roast, rib side down, in a shallow roasting pan. Insert meat thermometer into center of roast, not touching bone. Roast in a 325° oven, uncovered, for 1½ hours or till meat begins to brown. Remove from oven; cover loosely with foil to prevent stuffing from overbrowning. Roast for 1 to 1½ hours more or till meat thermometer registers 170°. Bake stuffing in casserole, uncovered, with roast the last 40 minutes of roasting. Garnish roast with fresh sage, if desired. Makes 8 servings.

Orange-Vegetable Pork Roast

Fines herbes is an herb blend used to season soups, stews, egg dishes, and meats. (Pictured on the front cover.)

1 **4-pound pork shoulder arm roast**
2 **tablespoons cooking oil**
1 **teaspoon finely shredded orange peel**
2 **cups orange juice**
2 **medium onions, quartered**
¾ **teaspoon fines herbes**
1 **bay leaf**
3 **medium sweet potatoes, peeled and quartered**
2 **cups fresh *or* one 10-ounce package frozen brussels sprouts**
1 **cup sliced fresh mushrooms**
¼ **cup cold water**
2 **tablespoons cornstarch**

● Trim excess fat from meat. In a large Dutch oven heat cooking oil. Brown meat in hot oil. Spoon off fat. Add orange peel, orange juice, onions, fines herbes, and bay leaf. Bring to boiling; reduce heat. Simmer, covered, for 1 hour.
● Add sweet potatoes. Cook for 20 minutes. Add brussels sprouts and mushrooms. Cook 15 to 20 minutes more or till meat and vegetables are tender. Transfer meat and vegetables to a warm serving platter. Keep warm.
● For sauce, remove bay leaf from pan juices. Skim fat from juices. Reserve *2 cups* of the juices (add additional water, if needed). Combine water and cornstarch; stir into the reserved juices. Return to the Dutch oven. Cook and stir till thickened and bubbly. Cook and stir for 2 minutes more. Serve the sauce with meat and vegetables. Makes 8 servings.

Pork Chop and Rice Bake

4 pork chops,
  cut ½ inch thick
1 tablespoon cooking
  oil *or* shortening
1 7½-ounce can semi-
  condensed cream of
  mushroom soup
½ cup water
½ cup dry white wine
⅔ cup long grain rice
1 4-ounce can sliced
  mushrooms, drained
1 teaspoon instant beef
  bouillon granules
1 teaspoon Worcestershire
  sauce
¼ teaspoon garlic powder
¼ teaspoon dried thyme,
  crushed
1 small onion, thinly sliced
  and separated into rings
  Snipped parsley

● In a 12-inch skillet brown chops on both sides in hot oil or shortening. Season with pepper.

● In an 8x8x2-inch baking dish combine soup, water, and wine; stir in *uncooked* rice, mushrooms, bouillon granules, Worcestershire sauce, garlic powder, and thyme. Top with pork chops, then add onion rings. Cover and bake in a 375° oven for 60 minutes or till chops are no longer pink. Sprinkle with snipped parsley. Makes 4 servings.

Pork Chops Dijon

These quick-to-fix chops get their spiciness from a mixture of Italian salad dressing, Dijon-style mustard, and pepper.

4 pork loin chops, cut ¾ inch
  thick
2 tablespoons Italian salad
  dressing
2 tablespoons Dijon-style
  mustard
¼ teaspoon freshly ground
  black pepper
1 small onion, sliced

● Trim excess fat from chops. In a small bowl combine salad dressing, Dijon-style mustard, and black pepper. Brush both sides of chops with mixture.

● In a 12-inch skillet cook chops, covered, over medium-low heat for 20 minutes. Turn chops. Add sliced onion. Cook, covered, for 5 to 10 minutes more or till meat is no longer pink. To serve, place chops on a platter; top with onions and pan juices. Makes 4 servings.

Roasting Fresh Pork

Cut	Approx. Weight (Pounds)	Internal Temperature on Removal from Oven	Approx. Cooking Time (Total Time)
Roast meat at constant 325° oven temperature.			
Center Loin Roast	3 to 5	170°	1¾ to 2½ hours
Sirloin Roast	3 to 5	170°	2¼ to 3¼ hours
Loin Blade Roast	3 to 4	170°	2¼ to 2¾ hours
Boneless Top Loin Roast	2 to 4	170°	1¼ to 2 hours
Tenderloin	1	170°	¾ to 1 hour
Shoulder Blade Boston Roast	4 to 6	170°	3 to 4 hours
Boneless Shoulder Blade Boston Roast	3 to 5	170°	2 to 3 hours
Shoulder Arm Picnic Roast	5 to 8	170°	3 to 4 hours
Leg (fresh ham)	12 to 16	170°	5 to 6 hours
Leg (fresh ham) rump portion	5 to 7	170°	3½ to 4½ hours

Roasting directions: Sprinkle meat with some salt and pepper. Place meat, fat side up, on rack in shallow roasting pan. Insert meat thermometer into center of roast so bulb reaches the thickest part of the lean meat. Make sure bulb doesn't rest in fat or touch bone. Do not cover, add water, or baste. Roast in 325° oven till thermometer registers 170°. To check, push thermometer into meat a little farther. If temperature drops, continue roasting. Let meat stand 15 minutes for easier carving.

Orange Pork Steaks

4 pork blade *or* arm steaks,
    cut ½ inch thick
    (2 pounds)
2 tablespoons cooking oil *or*
    shortening
4 medium sweet potatoes,
    peeled and cut lengthwise
    into ½-inch-thick slices
1 medium orange, peeled and
    thinly sliced
⅓ cup packed brown sugar
⅓ cup orange juice
⅛ teaspoon ground cinnamon
⅛ teaspoon ground nutmeg
    Fresh parsley sprigs
    (optional)

● Cut each pork steak into two serving-size pieces. In a skillet brown meat on both sides in hot oil or shortening. Sprinkle with salt and pepper. In a 12x7½x2-inch baking dish arrange sweet potatoes. Place orange slices atop potatoes; cover with pork steaks.

● For sauce, stir together brown sugar, orange juice, cinnamon, nutmeg, and dash *salt;* pour over steaks. Cover and bake in a 350° oven for 45 minutes. Uncover; continue baking about 30 minutes more or till meat is no longer pink and sweet potatoes are tender. Transfer to a platter; spoon sauce over steaks. Garnish with parsley, if desired. Makes 8 servings.

Oriental Glazed Riblets

To eliminate the fuss just before mealtime, include this tasty dish with built-in make-ahead potential on your menu.

3 pounds meaty pork
    spareribs, sawed in half
    across bones
1 15¼-ounce can pineapple
    chunks (juice pack)
¼ cup packed brown sugar
2 tablespoons cornstarch
¼ teaspoon salt
1 cup water
2 tablespoons vinegar
2 tablespoons soy sauce
1 medium orange, halved
    and thinly sliced
    Hot cooked pea pods
    (optional)

● Cut meat into two-rib portions. In a large saucepan or Dutch oven simmer ribs, covered, in enough boiling salted water to cover meat for 30 minutes; drain. Place ribs in a 13x9x2-inch baking dish. Season with salt and pepper.

● Meanwhile, drain pineapple chunks, reserving juice. In a saucepan combine brown sugar, cornstarch, and the ¼ teaspoon salt. Stir in the reserved pineapple juice, 1 cup water, vinegar, and soy sauce. Cook and stir till thickened and bubbly. Cook and stir for 2 minutes more.

● Stir pineapple chunks and orange slices into soy mixture. Spoon over ribs. Cover ribs and chill in the refrigerator for 3 to 24 hours.

● Bake ribs, covered, in a 350° oven for 20 minutes. Uncover; spoon pineapple mixture from bottom of baking dish over ribs. Bake, uncovered, 20 to 25 minutes more or till no longer pink. If desired, serve the ribs atop a bed of buttered cooked pea pods. Makes 4 or 5 servings.

Oriental Glazed Riblets

Hickory-Smoked Ribs

Most barbecued rib recipes are best done in a covered grill. To keep the ribs from burning, brush them with sauce only during the last 15 minutes of grilling.

Hickory chips
¾ cup catsup
½ cup finely chopped onion
¼ cup packed brown sugar
3 tablespoons prepared mustard
2 tablespoons wine vinegar
2 tablespoons Worcestershire sauce
1 teaspoon soy sauce
½ to ¾ teaspoon bottled hot pepper sauce
4 pounds pork loin back ribs *or* spareribs

● An hour before cooking, soak about 4 cups hickory chips in enough water to cover; drain.

● In a saucepan combine the catsup, chopped onion, brown sugar, prepared mustard, wine vinegar, Worcestershire sauce, soy sauce, and bottled hot pepper sauce. Simmer and stir for 10 minutes. Set aside.

● In a covered grill place *hot* coals on both sides of foil drip pan. Sprinkle with *one-third* of the dampened hickory chips. Grill ribs about 1 hour or till no longer pink. Sprinkle coals with dampened hickory chips every 20 minutes. Brush ribs with catsup mixture during the last 15 minutes of cooking. Pass the remaining catsup mixture. Makes 6 servings.

Using Your Broiler Instead of a Grill

To use a broiler instead of a barbecue grill, set the oven temperature to "broil"; preheat, if desired (check range instruction booklet). Broil pork 2 to 3 inches from the heat for half of the suggested time. Season with salt and pepper. Turn the meat with tongs, cooking until it's no longer pink. Season again.

Use the suggested grilling times in the recipe or follow these general guidelines for broiling pork: rib or loin chops (¾ to 1 inch thick), 20 to 25 minutes total time; shoulder steaks (½ to ¾ inch thick), 20 to 22 minutes total time; and pork kabobs (pieces about 1 inch square), 22 to 25 minutes total time.

Curry-Basted Pork Kabobs

1½ pounds boneless pork
4 large carrots
2 small zucchini
8 pearl onions, peeled
4 teaspoons curry powder
1 teaspoon paprika
1 teaspoon dried oregano, crushed
½ teaspoon salt
⅛ teaspoon pepper
1 clove garlic, minced
⅔ cup cooking oil

● Cut pork, carrots, and zucchini into 1-inch pieces. In a saucepan cook carrots, covered, in a small amount of boiling salted water for 15 minutes. Add onions; cover and cook for 10 minutes more.
● For sauce, in a small saucepan stir together curry powder, paprika, oregano, salt, pepper, and garlic; stir in oil. Heat through. Thread pork and vegetables onto six or eight skewers. Grill over *hot* coals for 10 to 12 minutes or till pork is no longer pink, turning once. Baste often with sauce. Makes 6 to 8 servings.

Chow Mein Pork Salad

This crunchy salad is easy to prepare and makes good use of leftover pork.

2 cups cubed cooked pork
1 cup shredded carrot
1 cup chopped celery
1 cup chopped green pepper
⅓ cup chopped onion
⅔ cup salad dressing *or* mayonnaise
1 tablespoon lemon juice
1 teaspoon prepared mustard
1 3-ounce can (2¼ cups) chow mein noodles
Lettuce cups

● In a mixing bowl combine cubed pork, shredded carrot, chopped celery, green pepper, and onion. Combine salad dressing or mayonnaise, lemon juice, prepared mustard, ¼ teaspoon *salt,* and dash *pepper;* add to meat and vegetable mixture. Mix well. Cover and chill. Add chow mein noodles just before serving; toss. Spoon into lettuce cups. Makes 4 to 6 servings.

Pork-Vegetable Skillet

1 pound boneless pork
2 tablespoons cooking oil
2 cups beef broth
1 medium onion, chopped
1 6-ounce package regular long grain and wild rice mix
2 stalks celery, thinly sliced
2 medium carrots, thinly sliced

● Partially freeze pork; cut on the bias into thin bite-size strips. In a large skillet brown pork strips in cooking oil; drain.
● Add beef broth, chopped onion, and seasoning packet from rice mix. Stir in rice. Cover and simmer for 10 minutes. Stir in celery and carrots; cover and simmer 15 minutes more or till meat is no longer pink and rice is done. Makes 4 servings.

Peppery Fried Rice with Pork

1 pound boneless pork
1½ cups quick-cooking rice
2 beaten eggs
1 tablespoon cooking oil
1 6-ounce package frozen
   pea pods
1 small sweet red *or* green
   pepper, cut into bite-size
   strips
1 clove garlic, minced
1 tablespoon cooking oil
⅓ cup sliced water chestnuts
3 tablespoons soy sauce
¼ teaspoon ground ginger
¼ teaspoon crushed red
   pepper

● Partially freeze pork; cut on the bias into thin bite-size strips. Set pork aside. Prepare rice according to package directions, *except* omit the salt. Meanwhile, in a 10-inch skillet cook the eggs in 1 tablespoon oil, without stirring, till set. Invert the skillet over a baking sheet to remove the cooked eggs; cut into short narrow strips.

● In the same skillet cook pea pods, red or green pepper strips, and garlic in 1 tablespoon cooking oil about 1 minute or till the pea pods are thawed. Remove from the skillet.

● Add more cooking oil, if necessary. Add *half* of the pork to the hot skillet. Stir-fry the pork for 2 to 3 minutes or till no longer pink. Remove from the skillet. Stir-fry the remaining pork for 2 to 3 minutes. Return all of the pork to the skillet.

● Stir in the cooked rice, egg strips, cooked vegetable mixture, water chestnuts, soy sauce, ground ginger, and crushed red pepper. Heat through. Pass additional soy sauce, if desired. Makes 6 servings.

Pork Stew with Cornmeal Dumplings

The robust seasonings in this hearty stew topped with double-corn dumplings also complement beef or lamb.

2 pounds pork stew meat, cut
   into 1-inch cubes
2 tablespoons cooking oil
1 28-ounce can tomatoes,
   cut up
1 12-ounce can (1½ cups) beer
1 medium onion, cut into thin
   wedges
1 tablespoon sugar
1 tablespoon Worcestershire
   sauce
1 teaspoon dried thyme,
   crushed
1 clove garlic, minced
2 bay leaves
¾ teaspoon salt
¼ teaspoon ground nutmeg
¼ teaspoon pepper
2 tablespoons all-purpose
   flour
   Cornmeal Dumplings
   Paprika (optional)

● In a 4-quart Dutch oven brown meat cubes, half at a time, in hot cooking oil. Return all meat to pan. Add *undrained* tomatoes, *1 cup* of the beer, onion, sugar, Worcestershire sauce, thyme, garlic, bay leaves, salt, nutmeg, and pepper. Bring to boiling; reduce heat. Cover and simmer for 1 hour or till meat is no longer pink. Spoon off fat.

● Stir together the remaining beer and flour; stir into stew. Cook and stir till thickened and bubbly. Prepare Cornmeal Dumplings. Drop batter by rounded tablespoons onto boiling stew mixture to make eight dumplings. Sprinkle tops with paprika, if desired. Cover and simmer, without lifting cover, for 10 to 12 minutes or till dumplings are done. Makes 8 servings.

Cornmeal Dumplings: In a bowl stir together ½ cup all-purpose *flour,* ⅓ cup *yellow cornmeal,* 1½ teaspoons *baking powder,* ¼ teaspoon *salt,* and dash *pepper.* Combine 1 beaten *egg,* 2 tablespoons *milk,* and 2 tablespoons *cooking oil.* Add to flour mixture and stir till blended. Stir in one 8¾-ounce can *whole kernel corn,* drained.

Peppery Fried Rice with Pork

Baking Smoked Pork

If you like, prepare a glaze for hams or other smoked pork roasts. At the last 20 to 30 minutes of baking time, spoon fat from the baking pan. Spoon the glaze over meat. Continue baking till the meat thermometer registers the desired internal temperature, basting occasionally with glaze.

Cut	Approx. Weight (Pounds)	Internal Temperature on Removal from Oven	Approx. Cooking Time (Total Time)
Bake meat at constant oven temperature of 325°.			
Ham (cook before eating)			
whole	10 to 14	160°	3¼ to 4 hours
half	5 to 7	160°	3 to 3¼ hours
shank or rump portion	3 to 4	160°	2 to 2½ hours
Ham (fully cooked)			
whole	10 to 14	140°	2½ to 3½ hours
whole, boneless	10 to 12	140°	3 to 3½ hours
half	5 to 7	140°	1¾ to 2¼ hours
half, boneless	5 to 7	140°	2 to 2¼ hours
Arm Picnic Shoulder (cook before eating)	5 to 8	170°	3 to 4 hours
Arm Picnic Shoulder (fully cooked)	5 to 8	140°	2½ to 3¼ hours
Canadian-Style Bacon	2 to 4	160°	1¼ to 2¼ hours

Baking directions: Place meat, fat side up, on a rack in a shallow baking pan. *Do not* cover or add water. Score ham fat in diamonds, cutting only ¼ inch deep. Insert whole cloves, if desired. Insert meat thermometer into center of thickest portion of meat, making sure bulb does not rest in fat or touch bone. Bake meat in 325° oven till meat thermometer registers the desired internal temperature. To check doneness, push the thermometer into meat a little farther. If the temperature drops, continue baking the meat to the desired temperature.

Ham with Pineapple-Orange Sauce

Cutting ¼-inch-deep slashes at 1-inch intervals around the ham slice before baking will keep it from curling.

1 **2-pound fully cooked ham center slice, cut ¾ inch thick**
2 **oranges**
1 **8-ounce can pineapple chunks (juice pack)**
 Orange juice *or* pineapple juice
4 **teaspoons cornstarch**
¼ **teaspoon ground cinnamon**

● Place the ham slice on a rack in a shallow baking pan. Bake in a 350° oven about 30 minutes or till heated through.
● Meanwhile, finely shred ¼ teaspoon orange peel; set aside. Cut the remaining peel and white membrane off the oranges; discard. Working over a small bowl, remove the orange sections by cutting into the center of the fruit between one section and the membrane. Then turn the knife and slide it down the other side of the section next to the membrane. Remove and discard any seeds. Repeat with remaining sections. Set the orange sections aside. Reserve the juice in the bowl.
● Drain pineapple, reserving juice. Stir reserved orange juice and pineapple juice together and add enough additional orange or pineapple juice to make 1 cup fruit juice mixture.
● In a medium saucepan stir together cornstarch, cinnamon, and orange peel. Add the 1 cup fruit juice mixture. Cook and stir over medium heat till thickened and bubbly. Cook and stir 2 minutes more. Gently stir in the orange sections and pineapple chunks. Pour fruit sauce over ham. Cover and bake 10 minutes more. Makes 8 servings.

Ham Bundles

Brushing the bundles with milk gives them a shiny, crisp crust.

1 **package (8) refrigerated crescent rolls**
1½ **cups ground fully cooked ham**
1 **medium apple, chopped**
½ **cup dairy sour cream**
2 **green onions, finely chopped**
1 **teaspoon prepared mustard**
 Milk

● Preheat oven to 425°. Unroll crescent roll dough; form into four 6x3½-inch rectangles by pressing perforated edges of two triangles together.
● In a saucepan combine the ham, chopped apple, sour cream, chopped green onions, and prepared mustard. Heat through over low heat; *do not boil.*
● Spoon one-fourth of the ham mixture onto half of each dough rectangle. Fold over the other half of the dough; seal edges with the tines of a fork.
● Place on an ungreased baking sheet. Brush bundles lightly with milk. Bake in the 425° oven about 10 minutes or till golden brown. Makes 4 servings.

Fiesta Ham Pie

2 cups fully cooked ham cut into strips
½ cup chopped onion
⅓ cup chopped green pepper
2 tablespoons cooking oil
2 tablespoons all-purpose flour
1 8-ounce can whole kernel corn
1 8-ounce can tomato sauce
¼ cup sliced pitted ripe olives
½ of a 1¼-ounce envelope (2 tablespoons) taco seasoning mix
1 8-ounce package corn muffin mix
½ cup shredded cheddar cheese

● In a large saucepan cook ham, onion, and green pepper in hot oil till onion is tender but not brown. Stir in flour. Stir in *undrained* corn, tomato sauce, olives, taco seasoning mix, and 1 cup *water*. Heat to boiling, stirring constantly.

● Prepare corn muffin mix according to package directions; stir in cheese. Pour tomato mixture into a 9x9x2-inch baking pan. Top with spoonfuls of muffin batter. Bake in a 375° oven for 25 minutes or till golden. Make 6 servings.

Bacon and Egg Sandwiches

6 hard-cooked eggs, chopped
12 ounces bacon, crisp-cooked, drained, and crumbled
1 cup mayonnaise
2 tablespoons curry powder
4 pita bread rounds, halved crosswise
2 tomatoes, chopped
4 cups shredded lettuce
½ cup alfalfa sprouts

● In a bowl combine eggs, bacon, mayonnaise, and curry powder. Spoon about *½ cup* of the mixture into *each* of the pita halves. Top with tomato, lettuce, and alfalfa sprouts. Sprinkle with salt. Makes 4 servings.

Leg of Lamb

Portion for roast leg of lamb comes from the hind leg. May be marketed in one piece, divided into sirloin and shank halves, or sold with roast or slices removed from the center.

Whole Leg of Lamb Whole leg consists of the full sirloin and the shank. It may also be boned, rolled, and tied. *Roast.*

American-Style Leg of Lamb is the whole leg with the shank bone removed. Meat is folded back into the pocket, squaring off the shank end. *Roast.*

Frenched-Style Leg of Lamb is the whole leg with meat trimmed off the shank bone end, making a handle for easier carving. *Roast.*

Center-Cut Leg of Lamb Roast cut from center of whole leg. *Roast.*

Leg of Lamb, Sirloin Half The half leg containing the full sirloin portion. The hip bone varies in shape throughout the cut. *Roast.*

Leg of Lamb, Shank Half The shank half or lower half of the leg. Contains the leg bone. *Roast.*

The small lamb carcass is usually divided into foresaddle (unsplit front half; includes ribs, shoulder, and breast) and hindsaddle (unsplit rear half; includes loin, flank, and legs). Usually the outer fat is covered by a natural, pinkish-red, papery layer called the fell, which may be removed if desired.

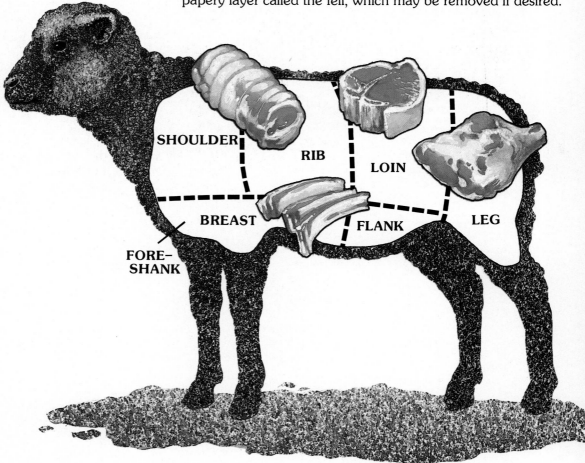

SHOULDER

RIB

LOIN

BREAST

FLANK

LEG

FORE-
SHANK

Lamb Roasts

Shoulder Blade Roast Cut from the upper shoulder area. Contains a section of blade bone, which varies in shape depending upon what part of the shoulder the roast is cut from. *Roast.*

Square-Cut Shoulder Roast Square-shaped cut with both arm bone and blade bone exposed. *Roast.*

Shoulder Arm Roast Cut from the lower shoulder area. Includes a section of the round arm bone. *Roast.*

Boneless Shoulder Roast A square-cut shoulder roast with the bones removed and the meat rolled and tied. Called a cushion roast when boned but left flat because its appearance resembles a cushion. *Roast.*

Rib Roast Cut from the rib or rack containing up to 7 rib bones. A **Rib Crown Roast** is two rib roasts, backbone removed, sewn with rib bones on the outside. Paper frills traditionally cover the bone ends when ribs are frenched. *Roast.*

Loin Roast Identified by T-shaped backbone and large top loin and smaller tenderloin muscles. *Roast.*

Lamb Chops and Steaks

Shoulder Blade Chop Cut from upper shoulder area. Contains blade bone, which varies in shape. May be boned, rolled, and skewered. *Braise, broil, panbroil, or panfry.*

Cubed Steak Mechanically tenderized boneless piece of meat. *Broil, panbroil, or panfry.*

Rib Chop From rib or rack. Has rib bone and rib eye muscle. Often frenched. *Broil, panbroil, panfry, or bake.*

Shoulder Arm Chop Lean chop from lower shoulder. Has arm bone. *Braise, broil, panbroil, or panfry.*

Leg Center Slice From the center of the leg. Identified by leg bone. *Broil, panbroil, or panfry.*

Loin Chop Cut from the loin. Identified by T-shaped backbone, large top loin or loin eye muscle, and smaller tenderloin muscle. A Loin Double Chop, often called English chop, is a cross-sectional slice from the unsplit double loin. *Broil, panbroil, or panfry.*

Leg Sirloin Chop From sirloin portion of the leg. Contains hip bone, which varies in shape. *Broil, panbroil, or panfry,*

Ribs and Shanks

Breast Spareribs Rib bones and cartilage. Most fat is trimmed off, leaving a thin covering of meat. *Braise, broil, or roast.*

Breast Riblets Made by cutting between rib bones. Alternate layers of rib bones, cartilage, lean meat, and fat. *Braise or cook in liquid.*

Lamb Shanks Cuts from the upper foreshank identified by the round arm bone. A very thin layer of fat covers the outer surface of the meat. *Braise or cook in liquid.*

Ground Lamb

Made from lean trimmings and the less tender cuts (shoulder and flank). *Bake, broil, panbroil, or panfry.*

Meat from the Breast

The breast is most often cut into riblets or stew meat, although large pieces are available for roasting.

Lamb Breast May be sold as roast for stuffing (has pocket between ribs and outer layers of meat). Also sold boned and rolled. *Braise or roast.*

Meats for Soups, Stews, and Kabobs

Lamb for Stew Lean meat cubes usually cut from the shoulder, breast, and leg areas. *Braise or cook in liquid.*

Lamb Cubes for Kabobs Boneless lean cubes from the shoulder and leg. Available in pieces or threaded on skewers. *Broil or braise.*

Sausage-Stuffed Lamb Roast

If you don't have time to bone a leg of lamb, order it boned and butterflied from your butcher.

1 6-pound leg of lamb, boned
and butterflied
½ pound bulk pork sausage
1 medium onion, chopped
1 clove garlic, minced
½ cup long grain rice
½ cup slivered almonds *or*
pine nuts
½ cup water
½ cup dry white wine
¼ cup raisins
1 teaspoon instant chicken
bouillon granules
¼ teaspoon ground nutmeg

● Pound lamb on the inner meat surface to ¾-inch thickness. In a skillet cook sausage, onion, and garlic till sausage is no longer pink. Drain off fat. Add rice and nuts to the skillet; cook and stir for 2 minutes. Stir in water, wine, raisins, bouillon granules, and nutmeg. Bring to boiling; reduce heat. Cover and cook for 12 to 15 minutes or till water is absorbed.

● Spread sausage mixture over lamb. Roll up jelly-roll style, starting from longest side. Tie with string. Place on a rack in a shallow roasting pan. Insert a meat thermometer into thickest part of meat. Roast in a 325° oven about 2 hours or till thermometer registers 170°. Makes 12 servings.

Glazed Lamb Chops

Here's an easy main dish you can have on the table in 20 minutes.

4 lamb loin *or* shoulder
chops, cut ¾ inch thick
¼ cup apple jelly
¼ cup chopped pecans
1 tablespoon lemon juice
¼ teaspoon ground
cinnamon

● Place lamb chops on a rack of an unheated broiler pan. Broil 3 to 4 inches from heat for 5 minutes. Season chops with salt and pepper. Turn; broil chops 3 to 5 minutes more or till tender.

● Meanwhile, combine jelly, pecans, lemon juice, and cinnamon. Spread jelly mixture over chops; broil 1 minute more. Makes 4 servings.

Lamb Shanks with Sauerkraut Sauce

4 lamb shanks (about 3½
pounds)
1 27-ounce can sauerkraut,
rinsed and drained
1 medium apple, sliced
1 medium onion, chopped
1 10¾-ounce can condensed
cream of mushroom soup
½ cup bottled barbecue sauce
¼ cup apple juice *or* cider
¼ teaspoon dried dillweed
1 bay leaf

● Place lamb shanks in a 13x9x2-inch baking dish. Bake, uncovered, in a 425° oven about 30 minutes or till brown. Remove shanks; drain off fat from baking dish.

● In the same baking dish layer sauerkraut, apple, and onion. Arrange lamb shanks atop. Combine condensed soup, barbecue sauce, apple juice, dillweed, and bay leaf; pour over lamb and sauerkraut. Bake, covered, about 1 hour or till meat is tender. Remove bay leaf before serving. Makes 4 servings.

Roasting Lamb

Plan on a little longer roasting time when a crown roast is filled with a stuffing.

Cut	Approximate Weight (Pounds)	Internal Temperature on Removal from Oven	Approximate Cooking Time (Total Time)
Roast meat at constant oven temperature of 325°			
Leg, whole	5 to 9	140° (rare) 160° (medium) 170° to 180° (well-done)	2 to 3 hrs. 2½ to 3¾ hrs. 3 to 4½ hrs.
Leg, half	3 to 4	160° (medium)	1½ to 1¾ hrs.
Square Cut Shoulder	4 to 6	160° (medium)	2 to 2½ hrs.
Boneless Shoulder	3 to 5	160° (medium)	2 to 3 hrs.
Crown Roast	3 to 4	140° (rare) 160° (medium) 170° to 180° (well-done)	1¾ to 2 hrs. 2 to 2¼ hrs. 2¼ to 2¾ hrs.

Roasting directions: Season the roast by sprinkling with a little salt and pepper. Insert a meat thermometer into center of roast so that the bulb reaches the thickest part of the lean meat. Make sure the bulb does not rest in fat or touch bone. Place roast, fat side up, on a rack in shallow roasting pan. *Do not* cover, add water, or baste. Roast in 325° oven till the meat thermometer registers desired internal temperature. To check doneness, push thermometer into meat a little farther. If the temperature drops, continue cooking meat to desired temperature. Let meat stand about 15 minutes for easier carving. Remove string from rolled and tied roasts; carve meat across the grain.

Broiling Lamb Chops

To check doneness, slit center of the chop and note the inside color: pink—medium; gray—well-done.

Thickness	¾ inch	1 inch	1½ inches
(approximate total time in minutes)			
Medium	10 to 12	11 to 13	15 to 18
Well-done	13 to 15	16 to 18	20 to 22

Choose lamb rib chops, loin chops, loin double chops, or leg sirloin chops. Slash the fat edge at 1-inch intervals to keep chops flat. Place chops on unheated rack in broiler pan.

Broil chops so surface of meat is 3 inches from heat (check range instruction booklet). Broil on one side for about half of the time indicated in the chart for the desired doneness. Season with a little salt and pepper, if desired. Turn with tongs and broil till desired doneness. Season again with salt and pepper.

Lamb Curry with Fruited Rice

2   slices bacon
2   pounds boneless lamb *or*
       pork, cut into 1-inch
       pieces
1   large onion, chopped
1   large apple, peeled,
       cored, and chopped
2   stalks celery, chopped
1   clove garlic, minced
1   tablespoon curry powder
½   teaspoon salt
½   teapoon ground cinnamon
1   cup water
1   cup dairy sour cream
2   tablespoons cornstarch
2   tablespoons snipped parsley
       Fruited Rice

● In a 12-inch skillet cook bacon till crisp; drain, reserving drippings in the skillet. Crumble bacon; set aside. Cook *half* of the meat in hot bacon drippings, turning to brown on all sides; remove meat and set aside. Repeat with the remaining meat; remove and set aside.

● Add onion, apple, celery, garlic, curry powder, salt, and cinnamon to the skillet. Cook and stir till onion is tender but not brown. Return meat to the skillet; add water. Cover and simmer about 1 hour or till meat is tender. Skim off fat.

● Combine sour cream and cornstarch; gradually add about ½ cup pan juices to sour cream mixture. Return all to the skillet. Cook and stir till thickened and bubbly. Cook and stir 2 minutes more. Transfer to a serving bowl. Sprinkle with bacon and parsley. Serve with Fruited Rice. Makes 6 servings.

Fruited Rice: In a saucepan combine 3 cups cold *water* and 1 teaspoon *salt;* bring to boiling. Stir in 1¼ cups long grain *rice,* ¼ cup snipped *dried apricots,* and ¼ cup *raisins.* Cover and cook over low heat for 15 to 20 minutes or till the rice is tender.

Herbed Meat-Vegetable Kabobs

½   cup cooking oil
1   medium onion, chopped
       (½ cup)
¼   cup snipped parsley
¼   cup lemon juice
1   teaspoon dried marjoram,
       crushed
1   teaspoon salt
1   teaspoon dried thyme,
       crushed
1   clove garlic, minced
½   teaspoon pepper
2   pounds boneless lamb *or*
       beef, cut into 1-inch
       cubes
4   medium onions, cut into
       wedges
3   medium sweet red *or*
       green peppers, cut into
       1-inch squares

● In a bowl combine oil, the chopped onion, parsley, lemon juice, marjoram, salt, thyme, garlic, and pepper; stir in meat cubes. Cover; refrigerate for 6 to 8 hours, stirring occasionally. Drain meat, reserving marinade. Cook onion wedges in water till tender; drain.

● Thread eight skewers with meat cubes, onion wedges, and sweet red or green pepper squares. Grill over *hot* coals about 15 minutes or till meat is tender, turning and brushing once with reserved marinade. (Or, place kabobs on a rack of an unheated broiler pan. Broil 3 to 4 inches from heat for 10 to 12 minutes or till meat is tender, turning and brushing once with reserved marinade.) Makes 8 servings.

Burgers Divan

3 slices bacon
¼ cup chopped onion
1 teaspoon Worcestershire
   sauce
½ teaspoon dry mustard
¼ teaspoon dried oregano,
   crushed
1 pound ground beef
¼ cup mayonnaise
2 teaspoons milk
4 slices tomato
1 small zucchini, thinly sliced
2 tablespoons grated
   Parmesan cheese
4 hamburger buns, split

● In a skillet cook bacon till crisp; drain, reserving drippings. Crumble bacon. Cook onion in skillet in reserved drippings till tender. Combine bacon, onion, Worcestershire sauce, mustard, and oregano. Add meat; mix well.

● Shape meat mixture into four ½-inch-thick patties. Broil 3 inches from heat to desired doneness, turning once (allow about 10 minutes total time for medium doneness). Combine mayonnaise and milk. Top each burger with a tomato slice and a few zucchini slices. Dollop burgers with the mayonnaise mixture; sprinkle with cheese. Broil about 1 minute longer. Serve on buns. Makes 4 servings.

Oriental Crunch Burgers

1 pound ground beef
¼ teaspoon ground ginger
⅓ cup fresh bean sprouts
¼ cup water chestnuts,
   chopped
2 tablespoons sliced green
   onion
1 tablespoon soy sauce
4 hamburger buns, split

● Combine beef, ginger, and ½ teaspoon *salt*. Shape into eight ¼-inch-thick patties. Combine bean sprouts, water chestnuts, green onion, and soy sauce; toss lightly. Place about 2 *tablespoons* sprout mixture on *each* of four patties to within ½ inch of edge. Top with remaining patties; seal edges.

● Place on rack of unheated broiler pan. Broil 3 inches from heat, turning once. For beef, broil to desired doneness (allow 10 minutes total time for medium doneness). For pork, broil 12 to 15 minutes or till well done. Serve on buns. Makes 4 servings.

Beef and Carrot Burgers

1 beaten egg
2 tablespoons milk
½ cup finely shredded carrot
¼ cup finely chopped onion
¼ cup wheat germ
¼ teaspoon dried marjoram,
   crushed
⅛ teaspoon pepper
1 pound ground beef
4 slices Monterey Jack cheese
4 hamburger buns, split
4 lettuce leaves
4 tomato slices

● In a mixing bowl combine egg and milk; stir in carrot, onion, wheat germ, marjoram, and pepper. Add ground beef; mix well. Shape into four ½-inch-thick patties.

● Grill patties over *medium-hot* coals to desired doneness, turning once (allow 10 to 12 minutes total time for medium doneness). During the last few minutes of cooking time, place a slice of cheese atop each patty. Serve patties on buns with lettuce and tomato. Makes 4 servings.

Beef and Carrot Burgers

Oriental
Crunch Burgers

Burgers Divan

Stuffed Burgers

1   beaten egg
3   tablespoons rolled oats
3   tablespoons sliced green onion
2   tablespoons catsup
1½   teaspoons prepared mustard
¾   teaspoon salt
⅛   teaspoon pepper
1½   pounds ground beef
1   3-ounce can chopped mushrooms, drained
6   slices American cheese (optional)
6   hamburger buns, split and toasted
6   lettuce leaves (optional)
12   tomato slices (optional)
   Sliced onion (optional)

● In a large bowl stir together the beaten egg, rolled oats, sliced green onion, catsup, prepared mustard, salt, and pepper.
● Add the ground beef. Use your hands to combine the mixture. Divide the meat mixture into 12 equal portions. Shape each into a ¼-inch-thick patty.
● Place mushrooms atop *six* of the patties to within ½ inch of the edges. Top with the remaining patties and press the edges together to seal.
● Grill patties over *medium* coals to desired doneness, turning once. (Allow 12 to 15 minutes total time for medium doneness.) *Or,* place patties on rack of unheated broiler pan. Broil 3 inches from heat to desired doneness, turning once. (Allow 10 minutes total time for medium doneness.) Top patties with cheese and continue heating just till cheese melts, if desired.
● Serve patties on buns with lettuce leaves, tomato slices, and sliced onion, if desired. Makes 6 servings.

Health Burgers

Use the leanest ground meat available for maximum good health.

½   teaspoon instant beef bouillon granules
⅓   cup hot water
¼   cup toasted wheat germ
½   teaspoon minced dried onion
1   pound ground beef, pork, lamb, *or* veal
1   cup shredded zucchini
1   cup alfalfa sprouts *or* wheat sprouts
¼   cup chopped walnuts
¼   cup creamy cucumber salad dressing
4   whole wheat hamburger buns, split, *or* 2 pita bread rounds, cut in half crosswise

● In a mixing bowl dissolve bouillon granules in hot water; stir in wheat germ and onion. Let stand a few minutes to moisten dried onion. Add ground meat; mix well. Shape into four ½-inch-thick patties.
● If using lamb or veal, melt 2 tablespoons *shortening* in a 10-inch skillet. In the skillet cook meat patties over medium-high heat to desired doneness, turning once. (Allow 8 to 10 minutes total time for medium doneness for beef or lamb; cook pork for 12 to 15 minutes total time or till meat patties are well done.)
● Meanwhile, for the sauce, combine the shredded zucchini, sprouts, walnuts, and salad dressing. Place patties on bottoms of buns or in pita bread halves; top each patty with some of the zucchini mixture. If using buns, top with remaining bun halves. Makes 4 servings.

Slaw-Topped Caraway Burgers

½ cup shredded cabbage
¼ cup finely shredded carrot
1 tablespoon mayonnaise *or*
  salad dressing
½ teaspoon prepared mustard
  Dash salt
1 beaten egg
1 tablespoon milk
⅓ cup soft bread crumbs
2 tablespoons chopped onion
¼ teaspoon salt
¼ teaspoon dried thyme,
  crushed
⅛ teaspoon caraway seed
½ pound ground pork *or*
  ground beef
2 hamburger buns, split and
  toasted

● For topping, in a mixing bowl combine the shredded cabbage, carrot, mayonnaise or salad dressing, mustard, and dash salt. Set the mixture aside.

● For burgers, in a mixing bowl combine the beaten egg and milk; stir in the bread crumbs, onion, the ¼ teaspoon salt, thyme, and caraway seed. Add ground meat; mix well. Form mixture into two ½-inch-thick patties.

● Place patties on a rack of an unheated broiler pan. For pork, broil 3 inches from heat for 12 to 15 minutes or till well done. For beef, broil 3 inches from heat to desired doneness, turning once (allow 10 minutes total time for medium doneness).

● Place the patties on the bottom halves of the buns; top each patty with *half* of the cabbage mixture. Add the top halves of the buns. Makes 2 servings.

Zucchini Burgers on Rye

1 slightly beaten egg
½ of a small zucchini,
  shredded (½ cup)
2 tablespoons finely chopped
  onion
¼ teaspoon salt
⅛ teaspoon pepper
½ pound ground beef
  Green goddess *or* creamy
  cucumber salad dressing
2 slices rye bread
½ cup alfalfa sprouts *or*
  shredded lettuce
2 tomato slices

● In a medium mixing bowl combine the beaten egg, shredded zucchini, chopped onion, salt, and pepper. Add the ground beef to the zucchini mixture; mix well. Shape the zucchini-meat mixture into two ¾-inch-thick patties.

● Place the patties on a rack of an unheated broiler pan. Broil meat 3 inches from heat to desired doneness, turning once (allow about 12 minutes total time for medium doneness).

● Spread the desired amount of salad dressing on each slice of rye bread. Top each slice with *half* of the alfalfa sprouts or shredded lettuce. Place one burger atop alfalfa sprouts or lettuce on *each* slice of rye bread; top *each* serving with a tomato slice. Makes 2 servings.

Pita Burgers

2 cups shredded lettuce
1 medium cucumber, seeded and finely chopped
1 8-ounce container plain low-fat yogurt
1 tablespoon sesame seeds, toasted
½ cup chopped onion
1 clove garlic, minced
1 teaspoon dried oregano, crushed
½ teaspoon salt
½ teaspoon dried basil, crushed
¼ teaspoon dried rosemary, crushed
1½ pounds ground beef *or* ground lamb
6 pita bread rounds

● In a small mixing bowl combine lettuce, cucumber, yogurt, and sesame seeds; set aside. In another mixing bowl combine onion, garlic, oregano, salt, basil, and rosemary. Add ground beef or ground lamb; mix well. Shape into six thin patties, each 5 inches in diameter.

● Grill patties over *medium* coals to desired doneness, turning once (allow 8 to 10 minutes total time for medium doneness). Slit each pita bread round to make a pocket. Place a cooked meat patty inside each pocket. Spoon in some lettuce-yogurt mixture. Makes 6 servings.

Ground Beef Labels

The labels on ground beef indicate the percentage of lean meat to fat. According to the standards set up by the meat industry, all ground beef must contain at least 70% lean meat. The standards also require that all ground beef contain exclusively beef and use no other meat trimmings, and that it contain no varietal meats. Ground round is the leanest ground beef, followed by ground sirloin and ground chuck.

Cheese-Stuffed Ham Patties

A rich mushroom sauce complements these succulent burgers.

 1 beaten egg
⅓ cup milk
½ cup fine dry bread crumbs
½ teaspoon dried oregano,
    crushed
½ teaspoon dried basil,
    crushed
¼ teaspoon pepper
½ pound ground fully cooked
    ham
½ pound ground pork
 3 slices mozzarella *or* Swiss
    cheese, torn up (3 ounces)
½ cup sliced fresh mushrooms
½ small onion, sliced
 2 tablespoons butter *or*
    margarine
½ cup milk
 1 tablespoon snipped parsley
 1 tablespoon all-purpose flour
½ cup dairy sour cream
 2 tablespoons dry sherry

● In a bowl combine the egg and the ⅓ cup milk. Stir in bread crumbs, oregano, basil, and pepper. Add ham and pork; mix well. Shape into twelve ¼-inch-thick patties. Place cheese on *half* of the patties to within ½ inch of edge. Top with remaining patties; seal edges. Place patties in a shallow baking pan. Bake in a 350° oven for 30 to 35 minutes or till done.

● Meanwhile, in a small saucepan cook mushrooms and onion in butter or margarine till tender. Stir in the ½ cup milk and parsley. Stir flour into sour cream; stir into mushroom mixture. Cook and stir till thickened and bubbly. Stir in sherry. Serve sauce over ham patties. Makes 6 servings.

Everyday Meat Loaf

 2 beaten eggs
¾ cup milk
½ cup fine dry bread crumbs
¼ cup finely chopped onion
 2 tablespoons snipped parsley
    (optional)
 1 teaspoon salt
½ teaspoon ground sage
⅛ teaspoon pepper
1½ pounds ground beef
¼ cup catsup
 2 tablespoons brown sugar
 1 teaspoon dry mustard

● In bowl combine eggs and milk. Stir in bread crumbs, onion, parsley, salt, sage, and pepper. Add ground beef; mix well.

● Shape meat mixture into desired shape. For an oblong meat loaf, pat meat mixture into an 8x4x2-inch loaf pan. For a round meat loaf, shape meat mixture into an 8-inch round loaf in a shallow baking pan. For a ring-shape loaf, pat meat mixture into a 5½-cup ring mold; unmold into a shallow baking pan. For individual loaves, pat meat mixture into 18 muffin cups.

● Bake meat loaf, uncovered, in a 350° oven (allow 1¼ hours for an oblong loaf, 50 minutes for a round or ring-shape loaf, and 20 minutes for muffin pan loaves). Spoon off excess fat. Combine catsup, brown sugar, and dry mustard; spread over meat loaf. Return to oven; bake 10 minutes more. Makes 6 servings.

Beef Sandwich Squares

Beef Sandwich Squares

1 pound ground beef
1 small onion, chopped
    (¼ cup)
¼ cup catsup
½ teaspoon salt
¼ teaspoon minced
    dried garlic
1 10-ounce package corn
    bread mix
1 8½-ounce can cream-style
    corn
¾ cup shredded American
    cheese (3 ounces)
2 eggs
2 tablespoons milk
½ cup shredded American
    cheese (2 ounces)
2 tablespoons cold water
2 teaspoons cornstarch
1 8-ounce can stewed
    tomatoes, cut up
2 tablespoons chopped,
    canned green chili
    peppers
1 teaspoon Worcestershire
    sauce

● In a large skillet cook the ground beef and chopped onion till the meat is brown and the onion is tender; drain off fat. Stir in catsup, salt, and minced dried garlic; set aside.

● In a bowl combine corn bread mix, cream-style corn, ¾ cup cheese, eggs, and milk. Stir just till combined. Spread *half* of the batter in a greased 8x8x2-inch baking pan. Spoon beef mixture over batter in pan; sprinkle with the ½ cup cheese. Top with remaining batter. Bake in a 350° oven for 30 to 35 minutes or till done. Let stand 5 minutes before serving.

● Meanwhile, for the sauce, in a small saucepan combine cold water and cornstarch. Stir in *undrained* tomatoes, chili peppers, and Worcestershire sauce. Cook and stir till thickened and bubbly. Cook and stir 2 minutes more. Cut corn bread mixture into squares. Spoon sauce over each square. Makes 6 servings.

Biscuit-Topped Stroganoff

1 package (10) refrigerated
    biscuits
1 3-ounce package cream
    cheese with chives
1 pound ground beef
1½ cups sliced fresh
    mushrooms
½ cup chopped celery
½ cup chopped onion
1 clove garlic, minced
3 tablespoons all-purpose
    flour
1 cup milk
½ cup dairy sour cream
2 tablespoons dry sherry
⅛ teaspoon pepper

● Flatten biscuits with your hand. Divide cheese into 10 portions. Place one portion in center of each biscuit. Fold in half. Press edges to seal. Cover; set aside.

● In a skillet cook ground beef, sliced mushrooms, chopped celery, chopped onion, and minced garlic till beef is brown and onion is tender; drain.

● Stir flour into meat mixture. Add milk, sour cream, sherry, pepper, and ½ teaspoon *salt*. Cook and stir till thickened and bubbly. Transfer to a 1½-quart casserole.

● Immediately top with biscuits. Bake in a 450° oven for 8 to 10 minutes or till biscuits are golden. Makes 4 or 5 servings.

Layered Meat and Potato Pie

A flaky piecrust encases savory ground beef and hash brown potatoes.

1 package piecrust mix (for two-crust pie)
½ cup milk
½ of a 1¼-ounce envelope (¼ cup) *regular* onion soup mix
   Dash ground allspice
   Dash pepper
1 pound ground beef
2 tablespoons snipped parsley
1 tablespoon butter *or* margarine, melted
1 12-ounce package (3 cups) frozen loose-pack hash brown potatoes, thawed
   Catsup, warmed

● Prepare piecrust mix according to package directions; roll out for a double-crust 9-inch pie. Line a 9-inch pie plate with *one* of the pastry circles; trim even with rim. Set remaining pastry circle aside. In a bowl combine milk, dry onion soup mix, allspice, and pepper. Add ground beef; mix well. Lightly pat meat mixture into the pastry-lined pie plate.

● Combine parsley and melted butter or margarine; add thawed hash brown potatoes, stirring to coat. Spoon potato mixture over meat layer. For top crust, cut slits in remaining pastry for escape of steam; place pastry atop filling. Seal and flute edge. Bake in a 350° oven about 1 hour or till crust is golden brown. Serve with warmed catsup. Makes 6 servings.

Meat-Noodle Casserole

3 ounces medium noodles (2¼ cups)
1 10¾- *or* 11-ounce can condensed soup
½ cup dairy sour cream
½ cup milk
½ cup thinly sliced celery
1 2½-ounce jar sliced mushrooms, drained
2 tablespoons chopped pimiento
1 tablespoon snipped parsley
1 pound ground meat, cooked and drained
   Seasoning (optional)
   Crumbs
¼ teaspoon paprika (only for bread crumbs)
1 tablespoon butter *or* margarine, melted

● Cook noodles in boiling water for 10 to 12 minutes or till tender; drain. Combine soup, sour cream, and milk. Add celery, mushrooms, pimiento, and parsley. Stir in cooked noodles, meat, and seasoning. Place in a 2-quart casserole. Combine crumbs and paprika (only with bread crumbs). Toss with melted butter; sprinkle over casserole. Bake, uncovered, in a 375° oven for 30 to 35 minutes or till hot. Makes 4 to 6 servings.

Soup suggestions: cream of mushroom, cream of celery, cream of chicken, cheddar cheese.

Meat suggestions: (cooked and drained): ground beef, ground pork, ground veal, ground lamb, ground raw turkey, bulk pork sausage.

Seasoning suggestions: ¼ to ½ teaspoon chili powder (with beef or pork); ¼ teaspoon dried basil, crushed (with any meat); ¼ teaspoon dried oregano, crushed (with pork or sausage); ¼ teaspoon caraway seed (with pork or beef).

Crumb suggestions: ¾ cup soft bread crumbs (1 slice), ¾ cup coarsely crushed corn chips or tortilla chips (omit butter), ½ cup finely crushed saltine crackers (14 crackers), ½ cup finely crushed rich round crackers (12 crackers).

Stuffed Green Pepper Cups

8 large green peppers
1 pound ground beef
½ cup chopped onion
3 medium tomatoes, peeled
    and chopped
1 8¾-ounce can whole kernel
    corn, drained
1 8½-ounce can cream-style
    corn
1 teaspoon salt
1 teaspoon dried basil,
    crushed
   Dash pepper
¾ cup soft bread crumbs
    (1 slice)
1 tablespoon butter *or*
    margarine, melted

● Cut tops from green peppers; discard seeds and membranes. Chop enough of the tops to make ¼ cup; set aside. Cook the whole green peppers, half at a time, in boiling water for 5 minutes; drain well. Sprinkle insides lightly with salt.

● In a skillet cook ground beef, onion, and the ¼ cup chopped green pepper till meat is brown and onion is tender. Add chopped tomatoes; simmer about 4 minutes or till tomatoes are cooked. Drain off liquid. Stir in whole kernel corn, cream-style corn, salt, basil, and pepper.

● Stuff peppers with the meat mixture; place in a 13x9x2-inch baking pan. Toss together bread crumbs and melted butter or margarine; sprinkle buttered crumbs atop peppers. Bake, uncovered, in a 350° oven for 35 to 40 minutes or till heated through. Makes 8 servings.

Stuffed Cabbage Rolls

1 beaten egg
½ cup milk
¼ cup finely chopped onion
1 teaspoon Worcestershire
    sauce
¾ teaspoon salt
   Dash pepper
½ pound ground pork *and* ½
    pound ground beef *or* 1
    pound ground beef
¾ cup cooked rice
6 large *or* 12 medium cabbage
    leaves
1 10¾-ounce can condensed
    tomato soup
1 tablespoon brown sugar
1 tablespoon lemon juice

● In a bowl combine egg, milk, onion, Worcestershire sauce, salt, and pepper; mix well. Add meat and cooked rice; mix well.

● Remove center vein of cabbage leaves, keeping each leaf in one piece. Immerse leaves in boiling water about 3 minutes or till limp; drain. Place ½ cup meat mixture on each large leaf or ¼ cup mixture on each medium leaf; fold in sides. Starting at unfolded edge, roll up each leaf, making sure folded sides are included in roll.

● Arrange in a 12x7½x2-inch baking dish. Combine soup, brown sugar, and lemon juice; pour over cabbage rolls. Bake uncovered, in a 350° oven about 1¼ hours, basting twice with sauce. Makes 6 servings.

Mexican Meat Cups

1 package (10) refrigerated
  biscuits
1 pound ground beef
1 15½-ounce can chili beans
1 15¼-ounce can Mexican-
  style sandwich sauce
¼ cup water
  Shredded lettuce (optional)
  Chopped tomato (optional)
1 cup shredded cheddar
  cheese (4 ounces)

● Roll or pat each biscuit into a 3½- to 4-inch circle; fit over the backs of well-greased muffin pans. Bake in a 400° oven for 8 to 9 minutes or till golden brown.
● Meanwhile, in a skillet cook meat till brown. Drain off fat. Stir in chili beans, sandwich sauce, and water; bring to boiling. Remove biscuits from pans. Fill with meat mixture. Sprinkle with shredded lettuce and chopped tomato, if desired. Top with cheese. Makes 5 servings.

Olive Spaghetti Sauce

1 pound ground beef
½ pound bulk Italian sausage
1 28-ounce can tomatoes, cut
  up
2 6-ounce cans tomato paste
1½ cups dry red wine
1 cup chopped onion
1 cup water
¾ cup chopped green pepper
3 bay leaves
2 cloves garlic, minced
1½ teaspoons Worcestershire
  sauce
1 teaspoon sugar
½ teaspoon chili powder
⅛ teaspoon pepper
1 6-ounce can sliced
  mushrooms
½ cup sliced pimiento-stuffed
  olives
  Hot cooked spaghetti

● In a Dutch oven cook ground beef and sausage till brown; drain off fat. Stir in *undrained* tomatoes, tomato paste, wine, onion, water, green pepper, bay leaves, garlic, Worcestershire sauce, sugar, chili powder, and pepper. Bring to boiling; reduce heat. Simmer, uncovered, for 2 hours, stirring occasionally. Remove bay leaves. Stir in *undrained* mushrooms and olives; simmer 30 minutes longer. Serve with spaghetti. Makes 8 servings.

Mexican Meat Cups

Skip-a-Step Lasagna

Uncooked lasagna noodles conveniently cook as the dish bakes in the oven.

1	pound ground beef
1	15½-ounce jar spaghetti sauce with meat
2	slightly beaten eggs
1½	cups cream-style cottage cheese (12 ounces)
⅓	cup grated Parmesan cheese
½	teaspoon dried basil, crushed
½	teaspoon dried oregano, crushed
9	lasagna noodles
1½	cups shredded Swiss cheese (6 ounces)
1	cup boiling water
2	tablespoons grated Parmesan cheese

● In a large skillet cook ground beef till brown; drain off fat. Stir in spaghetti sauce. In a mixing bowl stir together the eggs, cottage cheese, ⅓ cup Parmesan cheese, basil, and oregano.

● In a 12x7½x2-inch baking dish place *three uncooked* lasagna noodles. Spread *one-third* of the meat-spaghetti sauce mixture atop noodles. Top with *half* of the cottage cheese mixture and *½ cup* of the Swiss cheese.

● Repeat the layers of noodles, meat-sauce mixture, cottage cheese mixture, and Swiss cheese. Top with remaining three noodles and remaining meat-sauce mixture. Pour boiling water into baking dish around the edge. Cover tightly with foil.

● Bake in a 350° oven about 1 hour or till the noodles are tender. Uncover; sprinkle with the remaining Swiss cheese and the 2 tablespoons Parmesan cheese. Return to oven; bake 3 to 5 minutes more or till cheese melts. Let stand 10 minutes before serving. Makes 8 to 10 servings.

Pork Chop Suey

1	pound ground pork *or* ground beef
1	cup sliced onion
2	cups fresh bean sprouts *or* one 16-ounce can bean sprouts, drained
2	cups sliced fresh mushrooms
1	cup bias-sliced celery
½	of an 8-ounce can water chestnuts, drained and thinly sliced
⅓	cup chopped green pepper
1	16-ounce can chop suey vegetables, drained
1	10½-ounce can condensed beef broth
⅓	cup soy sauce
⅓	cup cold water
2	tablespoons cornstarch
	Hot cooked rice
	Chow mein noodles

● In a 12-inch skillet cook ground pork or ground beef and onion till meat is brown and onion is tender. Drain off fat. Stir in bean sprouts, mushrooms, celery, water chestnuts, and green pepper. Cook and stir for 2 minutes. Stir in chop suey vegetables, beef broth, and soy sauce. Bring to boiling; reduce heat. Cover and simmer for 2 minutes.

● Combine cold water and cornstarch; stir into vegetable mixture. Cook and stir till thickened and bubbly; cook and stir 2 minutes more. Serve over hot cooked rice; sprinkle with chow mein noodles. Makes 6 servings.

Chili

1 pound ground beef *or*
    ground pork
½ cup chopped onion
1 clove garlic, minced, *or*
    ⅛ teaspoon garlic powder
1 16-ounce can tomatoes,
    cut up
1 15½-ounce can red kidney
    beans, drained
½ cup beer *or* water
½ of a 6-ounce can (⅓ cup)
    tomato paste
2 to 3 teaspoons chili powder
½ teaspoon salt
½ teaspoon dried basil,
    crushed
  Chopped onion (optional)
  Shredded cheddar cheese
    (optional)

● Crumble the ground beef or pork into a large saucepan. Stir in onion and garlic or garlic powder. Cook over medium heat till meat is brown, stirring occasionally. Drain off fat.
● Stir in the *undrained* tomatoes, drained kidney beans, beer or water, tomato paste, chili powder, salt, and basil. Bring to boiling. Reduce heat. Cover and simmer for 20 minutes.
● Ladle into soup bowls. Top with chopped onion and shredded cheddar cheese, if desired. Make 4 to 6 servings.

Meal-in-a-Bowl Soup

1 pound ground beef *or*
    ground pork
½ cup chopped onion
3 10½-ounce cans condensed
    beef broth
1 soup can (1⅓ cups) water
1 10-ounce package frozen
    peas
2 large potatoes, peeled and
    cubed
1 cup sliced fresh mushrooms
1 large carrot, chopped
1 small zucchini, sliced
    (¾ cup)
1½ teaspoons dried basil,
    crushed
¾ teaspoon ground sage
½ teaspoon salt
⅛ teaspoon pepper

● In a large saucepan or Dutch oven cook ground beef or ground pork and onion till meat is brown and onion is tender. Drain off fat. Stir in beef broth, water, peas, potatoes, mushrooms, carrot, zucchini, basil, sage, salt, and pepper. Bring to boiling; reduce heat. Cover and simmer for 15 minutes, stirring occasionally. Makes 6 servings.

Lamb Pinwheel

¾ pound ground lamb
1 2-ounce can chopped
   mushrooms, drained
2 tablespoons chopped onion
2 tablespoons sweet pickle
   relish
1 tablespoon snipped parsley
   Dash pepper
1½ cups all-purpose flour
1½ teaspoons baking powder
½ teaspoon salt
¼ cup shortening
½ cup milk
   Sour Cream-Dill Sauce

● Combine lamb, mushrooms, onion, pickle relish, parsley, and pepper. Cover and cook over medium-low heat for 10 minutes, stirring occasionally; drain off fat. Stir together flour, baking powder, and salt. Cut in shortening till mixture resembles coarse crumbs. Add milk all at once; stir just till blended.

● On a lightly floured surface knead dough 8 to 10 strokes. Roll into a 10x7-inch rectangle. Spread with meat mixture. Starting at short side, roll up jelly-roll style. Seal seam. Place, seam side down, on lightly greased baking sheet. Bake in a 400° oven about 30 minutes or till done. Slice to serve. Pass Sour Cream-Dill Sauce. Makes 4 to 6 servings.

Sour Cream-Dill Sauce: In a saucepan stir 1 tablespoon all-purpose *flour*, 1 teaspoon dried *dillweed*, and ¼ teaspoon *salt* into ½ cup dairy *sour cream*. Stir in ½ cup *milk*. Cook and stir till thickened and bubbly. Cook and stir 1 to 2 minutes more.

Porcupine Meatballs

Grains of rice protrude from the meat, resembling quills of a porcupine.

1 beaten egg
1 10¾-ounce can condensed
   tomato soup
¼ cup long grain rice
2 tablespoons finely chopped
   onion
1 tablespoon snipped parsley
⅛ teaspoon pepper
1 pound ground beef
½ cup water
1 teaspoon Worcestershire
   sauce

● Combine egg and ¼ *cup* of the soup. Stir in the *uncooked* rice, onion, parsley, pepper, and ½ teaspoon *salt*. Add ground beef; mix well. Shape into 1-inch meatballs. Place the meatballs in a 10-inch skillet. Combine the remaining soup, water, and Worcestershire sauce; add to the skillet. Bring to boiling; reduce heat. Cover and simmer for 35 to 40 minutes, stirring often. Makes 4 servings.

Oriental Appetizer Meatballs

½ cup water chestnuts
2 cups soft bread crumbs
½ cup milk
1 tablespoon soy sauce
½ teaspoon garlic salt
¼ teaspoon onion powder
½ pound ground beef
½ pound bulk pork sausage

● Finely chop water chestnuts. In a bowl combine water chestnuts, bread crumbs, milk, soy sauce, garlic salt, and onion powder. Add ground beef and pork sausage; mix well. Shape mixture into ¾-inch meatballs. Bake in a shallow baking pan in a 350° oven about 20 minutes or till done. Makes 48 meatballs.

Types of Sausages

Sausages were favorite festival meats enjoyed by the Romans who gave them their name. Later "wurstmachers" developed dry and semi-dry varieties which kept well in warm climates; or fresh and cooked varieties in the cooler northern countries. Use these descriptions as a reference for the storage and cooking requirements of the specific sausage varieties listed on the next 3 pages.

Fresh

Made from uncured, uncooked meat. Some may be smoked. Treat like fresh meat. Keep refrigerated. Use within 3 or 4 days of purchasing. Cook thoroughly. Allow 4 or 5 servings per pound.

Uncooked, smoked

Made from cured meat. Smoking adds flavor and color. Keep refrigerated. Use within 1 week of purchasing. Most must be thoroughly cooked unless labeled "fully cooked," "ready-to-eat," or "do not cook." Allow 4 or 5 servings per pound.

Cooked

Made from fresh meats that may be either cured or uncured. Keep refrigerated. Use within 1 week of purchasing. Ready to eat. Generally served cold. Allow 4 or 5 servings per pound.

Cooked, smoked

Made from fresh meats that are smoked and fully cooked. Keep refrigerated. Use within 1 week of purchasing (2 weeks if unopened in original vacuum package). Ready to eat but usually served hot. Allow 4 or 5 servings per pound.

Dry, Semi-dry

Made from cured meats that are either smoked or unsmoked. Cured and dried through process of bacterial fermentation which develops characteristic flavor and also acts as a preservative. Allow 8 servings per pound.

Most **dry** sausages are salamis. The casings become shriveled and texture is very firm. Cool storage recommended. **Semi-dry** sausages are generally softer and include most cervelats. Keep refrigerated.

Prepared Meats

Cured meats are often thought of as sausages. May be smoked or unsmoked. Keep refrigerated. Use within 1 week of purchasing. Ready to eat; usually served cold. Allow 4 to 6 servings per pound.

Cooked Meat Specialties

Finely ground or pureed meat with spices and seasonings. Government regulates percentage of non-meat ingredients, such as cereal or dried milk, which can be added. May be cured.

Fully cooked or baked. Keep refrigerated. Allow 4 or 5 servings per pound. Typically called luncheon meats. Includes such items as olive loaf, pickle and pimiento loaf, old-fashioned loaf, honey loaf, peppered loaf and picnic loaf.

How to Cook

Fresh and uncooked sausages need to be thoroughly cooked before eating. Fully-cooked sausages may be cooked only until heated through if you want to serve them warm, or they may be served cold.

Uncooked Patties

Place in an unheated skillet. Cook slowly, uncovered, for 15 to 20 minutes or till thoroughly cooked, turning once. Drain well.
Or, arrange patties on unheated rack in a shallow baking pan. Bake in 400° oven for 20 to 25 minutes or till thoroughly cooked.

Uncooked Links

Do not prick. Place in an unheated skillet. Add ¼ cup cold water. Cover and cook slowly for 5 minutes; drain well. Uncover and cook slowly 12 to 14 minutes longer or till water has evaporated and sausages are thoroughly cooked, turning occasionally with tongs.

Fully Cooked Links

Add to boiling liquid (water, beer, or wine) in a saucepan. Reduce heat; cover and simmer for 5 to 10 minutes or till heated through.

Beerwurst

(cooked, smoked) Pork and beef; chopped. May be all pork. Seasoning includes garlic. Natural casings or bulk pieces for slicing. Also called Beer Salami.

Berliner Sausage *(cooked, smoked)*

Cured lean pork; coarsely ground. May include a small amount of beef or veal. Sugar and salt are the only seasonings. Packaged in slices or in bulk rolls for slicing. Variety known as Dutch Berliner adds bacon, eggs, onion, and spices.

Blood Sausage

(cooked) Pork fat cooked and diced;

cooked meat, finely ground; and beef blood. Spices include allspice, cloves, onion, salt, and pepper. May be smoked or unsmoked. Natural casings or bulk pieces for slicing. Also called Blutwurst, Blood Pudding or Long Blood Sausage, Pepper Blood (links), Bloodwurst, or Biroldo. Other varieties include Black Pudding (English) with added cereal; Boudin Noir (French) with brandy; and Toscano (Italian) with raisins.

Blood and Tongue Sausage

(cooked) Pork and/or lamb tongues are cooked and cured, then placed in center of **Blood Sausage.**

Bockwurst *(fresh or cooked)*

Veal, pork, milk, chives, eggs, and parsley. Seasonings similar to frankfurters. Generally available only from January to Easter. Popular at spring sausage festivals in Germany. Highly perishable. Light colored links about 5 inches long. Also called Swiss Sausages.

Bologna *(cooked, smoked)*

Beef and pork, finely ground and mildly seasoned. May also be all beef, or pork, or ham. Typical seasonings

include pepper, cloves, coriander, ginger, garlic, and nutmeg. Available in rings, chubs, and slices of varying diameters. Credited to Bologna, Italy. Many varieties depending on spices and meats used.

Bratwurst *(fresh or cooked)*

All pork, or pork and beef, or pork and veal. Spice formulas vary with the brand. German, meaning "frying sausage." Links often 1½ inches in diameter; usually 6 or 7 links per pound.

Braunschweiger

(cooked) Liver sausage that is smoked after cooking or includes smoked meats such as bacon. May also include milk and onions. Spices include coriander, ginger, marjoram, mustard, pepper, and salt. Smooth texture; may be sliced or spread. Credited to Brunswick, Germany. Available in various-size chubs and in whole pieces. Name may also be attached to other sausage types to indicate area of origin. (See also **Liver Sausage.**)

Cappicola *(prepared meat)*

Boneless pork shoulder seasoned with ground hot or sweet peppers, paprika, salt, and sugar. Smoked.

Cervelat *(semi-dry)*

Beef and pork; usually finely ground. Garlic is generally not included in the seasonings. Many varieties differentiated by grind of meat, spices used, and degree of smoking. Sliced or in rolls. Often given the general name **Summer Sausage.**

Chipolata *(fresh)*

Lean pork finely chopped, plus pork fat, coarsely chopped. May include rice and rusks plus salt, pepper, coriander, pimiento, nutmeg, and thyme. Links are usually 16 to 20 per pound. Italian; popular in France. Also called

Cipollata. Name sometimes used to mean very small sausages.

Chorizo *(dry)*

Pork, coarsely chopped and highly seasoned with pimiento, sweet red pepper, and sometimes garlic. Looks similar to **Italian Pork Sausage.** Spanish. Bulk and link forms.

Cooked Salami *(cooked)*

Cured pork and beef, but definitely has a softer texture than dry and semi-dry salamis. Many varieties.

Cotto Salami

(cooked, smoked) Pork and beef, coarsely ground, or all beef. Mild flavor characterized by whole peppercorns. May be smoked. Italian, meaning "cooked" salami. Sliced and in rolls.

Dried beef *(prepared meat)*

Beef round is cured, smoked, dehydrated, and thinly sliced.

Farmer Cervelat *(dry)*

Pork, coarsely chopped, and beef, finely chopped. Seasonings include mustard, pepper, salt, and sugar. Natural casings, usually about 2 inches in diameter. May also be called Farmer Sausage, **Cervelat,** or Bauernwurst.

Frankfurters *(cooked, smoked)*

Pork and beef, ground, or all beef. Typical seasonings include coriander, garlic or onion, dry mustard, paprika, nutmeg, salt, sugar, pepper, cloves, and mace. Credited to Frankfurt, Germany. Originally used beef and pork and had more seasonings (especially garlic) than wieners. Various sizes. May be skinless or with natural casings. (See also **Wieners**)

Fresh Polish Sausage *(fresh)*

Pork shoulder, coarsely chopped. Seasonings include garlic, marjoram, salt, sugar, and pepper. Usually in 10- to 14-inch links. (See also **Polish Sausage.**)

Fresh Thuringer *(fresh)* Pork or pork and veal; finely ground. May include dry milk solids, plus coriander, ginger, ground celery seed, mace, pepper, salt, and sugar. Usually in links, 3 to 5 per pound. (See also **Smoked Thuringer**.)

Frizzes *(dry)* Cured lean pork, sometimes with added cured lean beef; coarsely chopped. Some varieties made with hot spices; others with sweet spices. Irregularly shaped; natural casings.

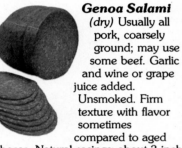

Genoa Salami *(dry)* Usually all pork, coarsely ground; may use some beef. Garlic and wine or grape juice added. Unsmoked. Firm texture with flavor sometimes compared to aged cheese. Natural casings; about 3-inch diameter. Credited to Genoa, Italy. May be called Italian or Hard Salami. Name may be attached to other sausages to indicate area of origin.

German Salami *(dry)* Beef and pork in equal amounts; coarsely cut. Seasonings are salt, pepper, garlic, and sugar. May be lightly smoked. Sliced or chub; about 3½-inch diameter. Also called Hard Salami.

Goteborg Cervelat

(dry and semi-dry) Pork and beef, coarsely chopped. Heavily smoked. Sweet flavor from the spice, cardamom; also tends to be salty. Described as a hard cervelat. Also called Swedish Sausage.

Head Cheese *(cooked meat specialty)* Chopped, cured pork head meat in gelatin base. Seasonings often include caraway, coriander, mustard, red pepper, salt, sage, and thyme. Colorful.

Holsteiner *(dry)* Similar in flavor and texture to **Farmer Cervelat** but has larger diameter and is often ring-shaped.

Italian Pork Sausage *(fresh)* Pork, coarsely or finely chopped. May include some beef. Seasoned with fennel, garlic, coriander, nutmeg, paprika, and sometimes red pepper. Bulk, sometimes links. Also called Salsiccia.

Italian Salami *(dry or semi-dry)* Usually cured lean pork; may have some beef. Seasonings often include garlic, cinnamon, cloves, nutmeg, salt, sugar, pepper, and peppercorns. May be moistened with red wine or grape juice. Never smoked. Includes many varieties.

Kielbasa—See **Polish Sausage.**

Knackwurst
(cooked, smoked) Beef and pork. Seasonings include coriander, garlic, nutmeg, salt, sugar, and pepper. Four-inch links usually served hot. German. Also called Knoblauch, Knochblauc, and Garlic Sausage.

Kosher Salami *(semi-dry)* Kosher beef, ground, plus cubes of fat. Seasonings include coriander, garlic, nutmeg, mustard, pepper, salt, and sugar. Meat and processing are under Rabbinical supervision.

Krakow *(cooked, smoked)* Lean pork, coarsely ground, and beef, finely chopped. Seasoned with pepper, garlic, salt, and sugar. Usually has 3-inch diameter. Polish and German. Similar to **New England Brand Sausage.**

Landjaeger Cervelat *(dry)* Beef and pork, or all beef with mustard, pepper, caraway, salt, and sugar. Heavily smoked and dried giving a black wrinkled appearance. Links are pressed to give flattened shape. Swiss.

Lebanon Bologna *(semi-dry)* Lean beef, coarsely chopped. Seasoned with cloves, coriander, garlic, ginger, pepper, salt, and sugar. Heavily smoked. Tangy flavor. Dark surface appearance. Credited to Pennsylvania Dutch in Lebanon, Pennsylvania. Sliced or in rolls.

Linguisa *(uncooked, smoked)* Pork, coarsely ground with garlic, cumin seed, and cinnamon. Cured in brine before stuffing. Portuguese.

Liver Cheese *(cooked)* Similar to **Liver Sausage** but with firmer texture. May be seasoned with coriander, ginger, mustard, onion, and pepper. Usually wrapped in white pork fat. Square shape, about 4 inches. Also called Liver Loaf.

Liver Sausage *(cooked)* Pork jowls and liver, finely ground. Smooth texture; slices or spreads easily. Seasonings include cloves, mace, marjoram, onion, salt, sugar, and pepper. Ring-shaped or in roll. Also called Liverwurst. One variety combines goose livers, diced pork tongues, and pistachio nuts.

Mettwurst
(uncooked, smoked) Cured beef and pork, finely chopped. Seasoned with allspice, coriander, ginger, mustard, salt, pepper, and sugar. Spreading consistency. German. Also called Teawurst or Smearwurst. Name may also be given to a semi-dry, coarsely ground sausage.

Mortadella *(dry)* Pork, finely chopped, plus cubed pork fat. May add beef. Seasoned with anise, coriander, garlic, and peppercorns. Italian. Natural casing.

Mortadella, German-Style *(cooked, smoked)* Pork and beef, finely ground, plus diced pork fat and pistachio nuts. Seasoned similar to a large bologna. Natural casing.

New England Sausage *(cooked, smoked)* Cured lean pork, coarsely chopped. May have cloves. Ham-like flavor. Large diameter rolls. Must be labeled New England-Style or -Brand when made outside New England.

Pastrami *(prepared meat)* Flat pieces of lean beef are cured, then rubbed with spices including garlic and cumin; smoked.

Pepperoni

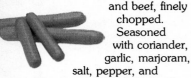

(dry) Beef and pork, coarsely chopped. Seasoned with red pepper and paprika. Sliced and in paired links, 10 to 12 inches long and about 1½ inches in diameter.

Polish Sausage *(cooked, smoked)* Pork, coarsely chopped, and beef, finely chopped. Seasoned with coriander, garlic, marjoram, salt, pepper, and sugar. May be uncooked. Links, 6 to 14 inches long; longer ones may be tied in ring shape. Also called Kielbasa, Kolbassy, or Kobasa. (See also **Fresh Polish Sausage**.)

Pork Sausage *(fresh)* Ground pork seasoned with pepper, nutmeg, and sage. Sold in bulk, patties, or links. Country-Style variety is mildly cured and may be smoked or unsmoked.

Potato Sausage *(fresh)* Beef and pork, finely chopped; mixed with potatoes. Seasonings include ginger, mace, onion, sage, salt, sugar, and pepper. Swedish.

Prosciutto *(prepared meat)* Ham that is dry-cured under pressure with spices rubbed in. Slice thinly.

Salami *(dry)* General category of highly seasoned sausages having a characteristic fermented flavor. Pork and beef with added garlic, pepper, salt, and sugar. May or may not be smoked. Sometimes called Dry or Hard Salami to differentiate from Cooked Salami which is more perishable. See **Cooked Salami, Cotto Salami, Genoa Salami, German Salami, Italian Salami,** and **Kosher Salami.**

Scrapple *(cooked meat specialty)* Ground cooked pork trimmings plus cornmeal. Other flours may be added. Seasonings include pepper, sage, and salt. Available in rolls or canned. To serve, slice and fry. Pennsylvania Dutch specialty. Also called ponhaws.

Smoked Sausage Links *(cooked, smoked)* Beef and pork, or all pork, coarsely ground. Seasoned with pepper; smoked. Size of links varies. Developed in Wisconsin in late 1940s.

Smoked Thuringer Links *(cooked, smoked)* Beef and pork, coarsely chopped. Seasonings include mustard, garlic, salt, sugar, and pepper. Usually 5 or 6 links per pound. (See also **Fresh Thuringer**.)

Souse *(cooked meat specialty)* Similar to **Head Cheese** but with a more sweet-sour flavor from addition of vinegar, pickles, and pimiento. Also called Sulze or Sylta.

Summer Sausage *(semi-dry, dry)* Properly used to describe all dry sausage, but especially refers to mildly seasoned soft cervelats such as **Thuringer Cervelat.** Originally made during the winter for summer use. Air drying removes much of the moisture giving them good keeping qualities. Typical lactic acid tartness.

Thuringer Cervelat *(semi-dry)* Beef and pork combination, or beef or pork alone. Mildly seasoned with coriander, pepper, cardamom, ginger, and mustard. Usually smoked. Often described as having the most tangy, fermented flavor of all cervelats. Credited to Province of Thuringia, Germany. Usually in rolls with about 2½-inch diameter. Name may be attached to other sausage varieties to indicate area of origin. (See also **Fresh** and **Smoked Thuringer.**)

Weisswurst *(fresh)* Pork and veal. Seasonings include mace, parsley, sage, thyme, lemon peel, salt, and sugar. Light color and delicate flavor. German, meaning "white sausage." Plump links about 4 inches long. Similar to cooked bratwurst.

Wieners *(cooked, smoked)* Beef, pork, and sometimes veal, finely chopped. Ratio of the meats used varies with the market price; most-used ingredient must be listed first on the label. Seasonings may include allspice, coriander, sugar, ginger, salt, and pepper. Credited to Vienna, Austria. (See also **Frankfurters**.)

Yachtwurst *(cooked)* Lean pork, coarsely chopped. May add beef. Includes pistachio nuts and garlic.

Polish Sausage-Kraut Skillet

1 medium onion, sliced
2 cloves garlic, minced
2 tablespoons butter *or*
   margarine
2 medium potatoes, peeled
   and sliced
1 cup sliced carrots
1 cup water
2 teaspoons instant beef
   bouillon granules
1 teaspoon sugar
1 teaspoon caraway seed
1 16-ounce can sauerkraut,
   rinsed and drained
5 precooked Polish sausages
   (about 1 pound)
2 teaspoons all-purpose flour
1 cup dairy sour cream

● In a 12-inch skillet cook the onion and garlic in butter or margarine till onion is tender but not brown. Stir in the potatoes, carrots, water, bouillon granules, sugar, and caraway seed. Bring to boiling. Reduce heat; cover and simmer for 10 to 15 minutes or till vegetables are tender.

● Place sauerkraut and Polish sausages atop vegetables. Cover; cook about 15 minutes more or till sausages are heated through. Stir flour into sour cream; stir into the sausage-kraut mixture and heat through. Season to taste with salt and pepper. Garnish with parsley, if desired. Makes 5 servings.

Italian Sausages in Brioche

1 package active dry yeast
⅓ cup warm water (110° to
   115°)
⅓ cup milk
⅓ cup butter *or* margarine
¼ cup sugar
¼ teaspoon salt
3 cups all-purpose flour
2 eggs, beaten
8 links Italian sausage
   (about 2 pounds)
3 tablespoons prepared
   mustard
2 slices cheddar,
   mozzarella, *or* Swiss
   cheese
1 egg white
1 tablespoon water

● Soften yeast in warm water. Heat milk, butter or margarine, sugar, and salt till warm (115° to 120°) and butter is almost melted, stirring constantly.

● Turn milk mixture into a bowl. Stir in *1 cup* of the flour; beat well. Add yeast mixture and eggs; stir till smooth. Stir in remaining flour. Scrape down sides of bowl, forming dough into ball. Cover bowl with plastic wrap. Refrigerate for 2 to 24 hours.

● Meanwhile, split Italian sausage links lengthwise. Place cut side down, on a rack in a shallow baking pan. Bake, uncovered, in a 350° oven for 25 to 30 minutes or till done. Drain on paper towels. Cool 30 minutes or till nearly room temperature.

● Spread cut sides of sausages with mustard. Cut cheese into eight 5x¾-inch strips. Place one strip on cut side of eight sausage halves. Top with remaining sausage halves, forming eight stacks.

● Remove dough from refrigerator. Punch down. Transfer to a lightly floured surface. Divide into eight equal portions. With floured hands or a rolling pin, flatten each into an 8x5-inch oval. Place one sausage link on each oval. Wrap dough around sausages, pressing edges to seal. Place seam side down on a greased shallow baking pan. Stir together egg white and 1 tablespoon water. Brush some egg white mixture atop each. Cover; let rise till nearly double (about 30 to 40 minutes). Bake in a 375° oven for 15 to 18 minutes or till golden. Makes 8 servings.

Polish Sausage-Kraut Skillet

Tacos in a Dish

1 16-ounce can stewed
tomatoes
1 teaspoon sugar
¾ teaspoon dried oregano,
crushed
½ teaspoon Worcestershire
sauce
Several dashes bottled hot
pepper sauce
¼ cup chopped green
pepper
¼ cup chopped onion
1 pound chorizo *or* bulk
Italian sausage
6 cups corn chips
4 *or* 5 slices American
cheese
2 cups shredded lettuce
Taco sauce (optional)

● In a mixing bowl stir together the *undrained* stewed tomatoes, sugar, dried oregano, Worcestershire sauce, bottled hot pepper sauce, ¼ teaspoon *salt*, and ⅛ teaspoon *pepper.*
● Using the edge of a spoon, break up large tomato pieces. Stir in the chopped green pepper and the chopped onion; set tomato mixture aside.
● In a medium skillet cook sausage till brown, stirring to break up large pieces of meat. Drain off fat.
● Coarsely crush corn chips; place in the bottom of an ungreased 8x8x2-inch baking dish or 8x1½-inch round baking dish. Spoon hot meat over corn chips; top with cheese slices.
● Bake in a 350° oven for 10 to 12 minutes or till heated through and cheese begins to melt. Sprinkle casserole with shredded lettuce; spoon on tomato mixture. Serve immediately. Pass taco sauce, if desired. Makes 4 to 6 servings.

Lasagna

1 pound bulk pork sausage *or*
ground beef
1 medium onion, chopped
1 clove garlic, minced
1 16-ounce can tomatoes,
cut up
1 8-ounce can tomato sauce
1 6-ounce can tomato paste
2 teaspoons dried basil,
crushed
1 tablespoon cooking oil
8 ounces lasagna noodles
2 beaten eggs
2½ cups ricotta *or*
cream-style cottage
cheese
¾ cup grated Parmesan *or*
Romano cheese
2 tablespoons dried parsley
flakes
1 teaspoon salt
1 pound mozzarella cheese,
thinly sliced

● In a skillet cook meat, onion, and garlic till meat is brown. Drain off fat. Stir in the *undrained* tomatoes, tomato sauce, tomato paste, basil, and 1 teaspoon *salt.* Cover; simmer 15 minutes, stirring often. Meanwhile, add the cooking oil to a large amount of boiling salted water; cook noodles in the water for 10 to 12 minutes or just till tender. Drain and rinse the cooked lasagna noodles.
● Combine eggs, ricotta cheese or cottage cheese, *½ cup* of the Parmesan cheese, parsley, 1 teaspoon salt, and ½ teaspoon *pepper.* Layer *half* of the noodles in a 13x9x2-inch baking dish; spread with *half* of the ricotta mixture. Add *half* of the mozzarella cheese and *half* of the meat sauce. Repeat layers. Sprinkle remaining Parmesan cheese atop.
● Bake in a 375° oven for 30 to 35 minutes or till heated through. (Or, assemble ahead and refrigerate; bake in a 375° oven about 45 minutes.) Let stand 10 minutes before serving. Makes 10 servings.

Easy Two-Crust Pizza

This lattice-top pizza is a specialty your friends aren't likely to forget!

1 16-ounce loaf frozen
    Italian, wheat, *or* white
    bread dough
¾ pound bulk Italian
    sausage *or* bulk pork
    sausage
¾ pound ground beef *or*
    ground pork
½ cup chopped onion
¼ cup chopped green pepper
    All-purpose flour
2 tablespoons yellow
    cornmeal
12 ounces sliced mozzarella
    cheese
¾ cup grated Parmesan
    cheese (3 ounces)
1 4-ounce can sliced
    mushrooms, drained
1 15½-ounce jar (1½ cups)
    extra-thick spaghetti
    sauce
    Milk
    Snipped parsley *or*
    grated Parmesan cheese

● Let the frozen loaf of bread dough thaw completely according to the package directions.

● Meanwhile, crumble the sausage and the ground beef or pork into a large skillet. Add the chopped onion and chopped green pepper. Cook and stir over medium heat till the meat is browned and the onion and pepper are tender. Drain off fat.

● Set aside one-third of the bread dough. On a lightly floured surface roll the remaining bread dough into a 14-inch circle. (If the dough becomes too elastic, let it stand for a few minutes for easier rolling.) Grease a 12-inch pizza pan; sprinkle it with the cornmeal. Fit the dough into the pizza pan, pressing the edge of the dough just over the edge of the pan.

● On a lightly floured surface roll the reserved one-third of the bread dough into a 14x8-inch rectangle. Cut into eight 14x1-inch strips; set aside.

● Arrange *half* of the mozzarella cheese slices atop the circle of bread dough in the pizza pan. Spoon the meat mixture atop the mozzarella cheese. Top with the ¾ cup grated Parmesan cheese and the drained, sliced mushrooms. Spoon the spaghetti sauce atop and top with the remaining mozzarella cheese slices.

● Brush dough strips with milk; sprinkle with parsley or Parmesan cheese. To make a lattice top on the pizza, lay four strips of bread dough on the filled pizza all in one direction. Lay the remaining four strips across the first four at a 90-degree angle. Cut off the excess dough beyond the edges of the pan. Pinch the edges of the strips to the bottom crust to seal. Press the edges toward the center to hold in the filling.

● Bake in a 400° oven for 25 to 30 minutes or till the crust is golden and the filling is bubbly. Makes 8 servings.

Sausage Sandwiches

1 pound bulk Italian sausage
½ pound ground beef
1 medium onion, chopped
1 15-ounce can tomato sauce
1 7½-ounce can tomatoes,
    cut up
1 teaspoon dried oregano,
    crushed
4 individual French rolls
    (about 8 inches long)
1 6-ounce package (4 slices)
    mozzarella cheese slices

● In a 10-inch skillet cook sausage, beef, and onion till meat is brown; drain off fat. Stir in tomato sauce, *undrained* tomatoes, oregano, ¾ teaspoon *salt*, and ⅛ teaspoon *pepper*. Bring to boiling. Reduce heat and simmer, uncovered, about 25 minutes or till mixture is thick, stirring frequently.

● Slice the French rolls lengthwise, cutting almost all of the way through. Spoon in the meat mixture. Top with mozzarella cheese. Place the rolls on a 15x10x1-inch baking pan. Bake in a 400° oven for 6 to 8 minutes or till cheese is melted. Cut rolls in half crosswise. Makes 8 servings.

Chili-Cheese Franks

1 15½-ounce can chili with
beans
½ of an 11-ounce can
condensed cheddar
cheese soup
2 teaspoons minced dried
onion
1 pound frankfurters
(8 to 10)
8 to 10 frankfurter
buns, split and
toasted
1 to 1½ cups corn chips
or tortilla chips,
coarsely crushed

● In a large saucepan combine chili with beans, cheese soup, and minced dried onion. Add frankfurters; bring to boiling. Reduce heat; simmer, uncovered, about 5 minutes.

● To serve, place a frank in each toasted bun. Top with chili-cheese mixture and sprinkle with coarsely crushed corn chips or tortilla chips. Makes 4 or 5 servings.

Spicy Frankfurter Soup

The little bit of chili powder and the dash of hot pepper sauce add zest to this soup.

1 pound frankfurters
(8 to 10)
1 large onion, chopped
(1 cup)
2 stalks celery, sliced
(1 cup)
1 small green pepper,
chopped (½ cup)
2 tablespoons butter
or margarine
1 16-ounce can refried
beans
¼ teaspoon pepper
¼ teaspoon chili powder
⅛ teaspoon minced dried
garlic
Several dashes bottled hot
pepper sauce (optional)
1 10¾-ounce can condensed
chicken broth
1 8¾-ounce can whole kernel
corn
½ cup water
Shredded cheddar cheese
Chopped tomato
Tortilla chips

● Thinly slice frankfurters; set aside. In a 3-quart saucepan cook onion, celery, and green pepper in butter or margarine till tender. Add refried beans, pepper, chili powder, minced dried garlic, and hot pepper sauce, if desired. Stir in chicken broth, *undrained* corn, water, and sliced frankfurters.

● Bring frankfurter mixture to boiling. Reduce heat; cover and simmer for 10 minutes. Serve in soup bowls; pass shredded cheese, chopped tomato, and tortilla chips to sprinkle atop each serving. Makes 5 servings.

Variety meats include the organs and other nonfleshy parts of a meat animal used for food. They're usually removed before the meat is divided into wholesale cuts; retail stores must order them specially. All are very perishable and so are best cooked the same day purchased. Liver, heart, and kidneys are ready to cook after the meat is trimmed and any membranes or veins have been removed. Tongue, tripe, chitterlings, and usually sweetbreads and brains are simmered in water before completing cooking. Since variety meats are boneless, you can plan on 4 servings per pound when served as the meat course, or 6 servings per pound when served in creamed dishes with eggs or cheese.

Liver

Best known and most popular of the variety meats. Most of the liver sold is beef or baby beef (calf) liver. Pork, veal, and lamb livers are less common. Livers differ slightly in taste, with beef and pork livers generally more flavorful than baby beef, veal, or lamb livers. Prepare for cooking by removing any tough outer membrane (usually, the retailer has already removed this membrane for

you). Also, cut out any veins or hard portions that are present. Then cut into thin slices. Beef liver is usually

panfried, allowing only 2 to 3 minutes per side so as not to overcook. Pork liver is always cooked well-done and often braised to keep the meat moist. Lamb and veal livers are tender enough for broiling. Brush the surface with bacon drippings or melted butter to keep the meat from drying out.

Kidneys

Organ meats taken from the loin sections of beef, pork, lamb, and veal. Kidneys range in flavor from delicate lamb, through veal and pork, to beef, which has the most pronounced taste.

Prepare for cooking by removing any membranes and white hard portions from the center of kidneys. Cook beef kidneys in liquid about 2 hours, or braise.

Braise pork kidneys to assure thorough cooking. Lamb and veal kidneys are tender enough for broiling. Because of their small size, lamb kidneys are usually served whole.

Sweetbreads

The thymus glands from the neck or throat of young animals, usually beef. Although not widely available, some sweetbreads also come from the pancreas. Sweetbreads have a delicate flavor, and are often the most expensive of the variety meats. Cook

by simmering in a covered pan of salted water about 20 minutes or till tender. Add vinegar or lemon juice to the cooking water to keep sweetbreads white and firm. Remove the thin membrane coverings.

Sweetbreads may then be broiled, sliced and panfried, or served in creamed mixtures.

Tripe

Actually the stomach lining from beef. Honeycomb is the preferred type. It has the lacy construction of a honeycomb and is more delicate than the plain variety. Plain tripe is smooth and somewhat rubbery in texture. Tripe is available fresh, canned, and pickled. Cook fresh tripe as a whole piece or cut into strips or serving-size pieces.

Simmer, covered, in salted water till tripe has a clear, jellylike appearance. Then fry; broil, basting with butter; or use in a prepared dish.

Brains

Have a delicate flavor and soft consistency. Before cooking, cover brains with cold water. Add a small amount of vinegar or lemon juice to the water to keep the meat firm and white. Soak for 30 minutes; drain. Remove the loose fatty membrane. Simmer brains in enough salted water to cover for 20 to 30 minutes. May then be broiled, panfried, or cooked with another food. Cooked brains are often cut up and scrambled with eggs or served in a white sauce.

Heart

Beef heart is the largest and most commonly sold. It is usually cut or split. The meat is firm, resembling typical muscle meat. Prepare for cooking by cutting out any hard portions such as arteries, and trimming off any fat. Leave whole or slice. The heart is a hard-working muscle. Consequently, it is one of the less tender cuts of meat. This means that it requires slow, moist-heat cooking to give a tender product. Heart may be braised or simmered, covered, in a large amount of liquid until tender. Or stuff the heart and bake, covered, with added liquid.

Tongue

Most tongue sold is beef, which may be fresh, pickled, or smoked. The flavor and texture of fresh beef tongue are similar to a fine-grained beef roast. Pork and lamb tongues are used in blood and tongue sausage. Tongue is not a tender meat and needs long, slow cooking in liquid to make it tender. Cook fresh tongue by simmering, covered, in enough salted water to cover until tender. Seasonings may be added to the cooking water. Allow a cooking time of about 1 hour per pound of meat. Cut away any gristle. Slit the skin lengthwise and peel off. Thinly slice meat and serve hot or cold. If planning to serve cold, cool tongue in cooking liquid in the refrigerator to retain juiciness.

Chitterlings

The small intestines of a pig. They're used in some regional dishes, especially in the South. Also called chitlins. Available cleaned, frozen, and ready to cook, or canned and ready to eat. If using fresh chitterlings, trim away any fat. Simmer in water for 2 to 3 hours or until tender. Seasonings may be added to the cooking water. Cooked chitterlings may then be panfried or deep-fat fried for serving.

Cheesy Broccoli-Liver Bake

1   pound sliced beef liver
¼   cup all-purpose flour
2   tablespoons butter *or*
    margarine
1   4-ounce can mushroom
    stems and pieces, drained,
    or 1 cup sliced fresh
    mushrooms
½   cup chopped onion
2   tablespoons butter *or*
    margarine
2   tablespoons all-purpose
    flour
¼   teaspoon salt
    Dash pepper
1½   cups *reconstituted* nonfat
    dry milk *or* milk
½   cup shredded American *or*
    Swiss cheese (2 ounces)
1   10-ounce package frozen
    cut broccoli, cooked and
    drained
¼   cup fine dry bread crumbs
¼   cup grated Parmesan cheese
2   tablespoons snipped parsley
2   tablespoons butter *or*
    margarine, melted

● Cut liver into four serving-size pieces. Sprinkle liver with a little salt and pepper; coat with ¼ cup flour.

● In a large skillet melt 2 tablespoons butter or margarine. Add liver; cook quickly about 5 minutes or till browned, turning once. Remove liver; set aside. In the same skillet cook the mushrooms and onion about 3 minutes or till onion is tender but not brown, adding more butter or margarine, if necessary. Remove from heat; set aside.

● In a saucepan melt 2 tablespoons butter or margarine; blend in the 2 tablespoons flour, salt, and pepper. Add milk all at once. Cook and stir till thickened and bubbly. Stir in American or Swiss cheese. Stir broccoli into *1 cup* of the cheese sauce; set aside remaining cheese sauce.

● Pour broccoli mixture into the bottom of a 10x6x2-inch baking dish; top with liver and cooked mushroom-onion mixture. Pour remaining cheese sauce over all. Combine bread crumbs, Parmesan cheese, parsley, and 2 tablespoons melted butter or margarine. Sprinkle over sauce. Bake in a 350° oven for 25 to 30 minutes or till heated through. Makes 4 servings.

Creole Liver Skillet

2   to 4 slices bacon
1   small onion, sliced
¼   cup chopped green pepper
1   pound sliced beef liver, cut
    into bite-size pieces
1   16-ounce can tomatoes, cut
    up
1   teaspoon lemon juice
1   teaspoon Worcestershire
    sauce
1   teaspoon prepared mustard
½   teaspoon salt
1   tablespoon cornstarch
1   tablespoon cold water
    Hot cooked rice

● In a 10-inch skillet cook bacon till crisp; drain, reserving 2 tablespoons drippings in skillet. Crumble bacon; set aside.

● Cook onion and green pepper in reserved drippings till onion is tender but not brown; push to one side of skillet. Add liver. Cook quickly for 2 to 3 minutes or till browned.

● Add *undrained* tomatoes, lemon juice, Worcestershire sauce, mustard, salt, and ¼ teaspoon *pepper*. Cover and simmer for 2 to 3 minutes. Blend cornstarch and water; add to liver mixture in skillet. Cook and stir till thickened and bubbly. Serve over hot cooked rice; sprinkle with bacon. Makes 4 to 5 servings.

Tongue and Lima Skillet

2 tablespoons chopped onion
1 tablespoon butter *or*
   margarine
1⅓ cups water
1 10-ounce package frozen
   baby lima beans
1 teaspoon instant beef
   bouillon granules
1 teaspoon Worcestershire
   sauce
¼ teaspoon dried thyme,
   crushed
⅓ cup catsup
1 tablespoon cornstarch
12 ounces thinly sliced
   cooked tongue

● In a 10-inch skillet cook onion in butter or margarine till tender but not brown. Stir in water, lima beans, bouillon granules, Worcestershire sauce, and thyme. Bring to boiling. Reduce heat; simmer, covered, for 10 minutes.

● Stir catsup into cornstarch. Stir into *undrained* lima bean mixture. Cook and stir till thickened and bubbly. Cook and stir 1 to 2 minutes more. Stir in the sliced tongue; cook till heated through. Makes 4 servings.

Kidney in Herb Sauce

This colorful entrée will remind you of Beef Stroganoff.

¾ to 1 pound beef kidney
2 cups water
½ cup chopped onion
1 small clove garlic, minced
1 tablespoon instant beef
   bouillon granules
½ teaspoon dried thyme,
   crushed
¼ teaspoon salt
½ cup coarsely chopped carrot
½ cup coarsely chopped celery
½ cup dairy sour cream
3 tablespoons all-purpose
   flour
   Hot cooked noodles
   Snipped parsley (optional)

● Remove membranes and hard parts from kidney; cut meat crosswise into ½-inch strips. Combine kidney strips, water, chopped onion, garlic, beef bouillon granules, thyme, and salt. Cover; cook over low heat for 1½ hours, stirring occasionally.

● Stir in carrot and celery. Cover and continue cooking about 25 minutes more or till kidney and vegetables are tender.

● Remove vegetables and kidney; keep warm. Strain pan juices. Add water to juices, if necessary, to make 1½ cups liquid. Blend together sour cream and flour; stir some of the hot liquid into sour cream mixture. Return all to pan. Cook and stir till thickened; *do not boil*. Return vegetables and kidney to pan; heat through. Serve over hot cooked noodles. Garnish with snipped parsley, if desired. Makes 4 servings.

MEAT GUIDE

The following eight pages present an assortment of information that will help you understand meat terminology and make the best meat buys. In addition to specific buying guides and preparation tips, you'll find a dictionary of meat terms, carving instructions, recipes for beef stock and pan gravy, and a guide to recommended storage times.

Meat Terms

Aging An expensive process used on high quality beef. Wholesale or retail cuts of beef are hung to dry in a temperature-controlled, low-humidity cooler for from 2 to 6 weeks. During the aging process, enzymes break down some of the tendons and fibers in the meat, thus making the meat more tender. At the same time, evaporation of liquids in the meat causes the meat to become firmer and to shrink. This shrinkage results in increased cost per pound of meat.

Au jus Served in natural meat juices from roasting.

Bake To cook covered or uncovered in an oven or an oven-type appliance.

Baste To moisten foods during cooking with pan drippings or a special sauce to add flavor and to help prevent the food from drying out during cooking.

Boil To cook in liquid at boiling temperature (212°F. at sea level) where bubbles rise to the surface and break. In a full rolling boil, bubbles form rapidly throughout the mixture.

Braise To cook slowly with a small amount of liquid in a tightly covered pan on range top or in oven.

Bread To coat with bread crumbs before cooking.

Broil To cook by direct heat, usually in broiler.

Butterfly To split almost entirely and spread apart, making flat piece.

Dice To cut food in small cubes of uniform size.

Dredge To sprinkle or coat with flour or other fine substance.

Filet A strip of lean meat.

Frenching Trimming a small amount of meat from end of a bone.

Fry To cook a food in hot fat. **Pan-frying** is to cook food in a small amount of shortening or other fat. **Deep-fat frying** is to cook food immersed in large amount of cooking oil or other fat.

Garnish To trim with small pieces of colorful foods such as green pepper, pimiento, or lemon.

Julienne Match-like strips of vegetables, fruits, or meats.

Larding Adding fat to meat before it is cooked. Specifically used in French cooking, it refers to inserting narrow strips of fat into a piece of meat—a roast, for example—at equal intervals.

London broil A thin steak that is broiled and then carved in very thin diagonal slices. A flank steak is the cut most commonly used.

Marbling The interior fat in meat that is recognizable as streaks of white interspersed in the red meat fibers.

Marinate To add flavor to food by allowing it to stand in a liquid.

Mince To chop food into extremely small pieces.

Panbroil To cook uncovered on a hot surface, such as a skillet, removing fat as it accumulates.

Pounding A tenderizing method in which a wooden or metal mallet is used to strike heavy repeated blows on the surface of meat.

Roast To cook uncovered without water added, usually in an oven.

Roux A mixture of flour and fat that is cooked, sometimes till the flour browns, and used to thicken soups and sauces.

Sauté To brown or cook in a small amount of hot fat.

Score To cut narrow grooves or slits into the outer surface of food, making a diamond pattern.

Sear To brown the surface of meat very quickly by cooking over intense heat. Recent tests have questioned the old theory that this helps to seal in meat juices.

Simmer To cook food in liquid over low heat at a temperature below boiling (185° to 210°F.) where bubbles form at a slow rate and burst before reaching the surface.

Stew To simmer slowly in a small amount of liquid.

Type of Meat	Servings Per Pound
Boneless meat (ground, stew, or variety meats)	4 or 5
Cuts with little bone (beef round or ham center cuts, lamb or veal cutlets)	3 or 4
Cuts with medium amount of bone (whole or end cuts of beef round, bone-in ham; loin, rump, rib, or chuck roasts; steaks, chops)	2 or 3
Cuts with much bone (shank, spareribs, short ribs)	1 or 2

In addition to price per serving, also consider the following things. Do you plan to serve only one meal from a particular cut? (Leftovers can become planned-overs with a little forethought.) What kinds and amounts of food are you serving with the meat? Do the people you plan to serve have light or hearty appetites? (Age makes a difference; so does activity level.) Do you have adequate refrigerator or freezer storage? How much time do you have for preparation? (A roast will take longer than ground beef.)

How Much to Buy

Price per pound is what you see, but price per serving is what you want to consider. A boneless piece of meat that is well trimmed of fat may be priced higher per pound but actually cost less per serving because there's more edible meat. This guide to servings per pound will help you comparison-shop.

Beef is sold by the hanging or gross weight. You pay for the entire weight of the carcass before cutting, including bones and fat. As a general rule, a beef carcass will give 25% ground beef or stew meat, 25% steaks, 25% roasts, and 25% waste.

If you are buying a quarter, you'll note that the hindquarter will be more costly per pound than either a forequarter or half, but it contains the loin and round where many tender steaks and roasts are located. The majority of the cheaper forequarter is made up of less tender cuts. Sometimes you can save more by watching the supermarket specials for pot roasts and ground beef than by purchasing a forequarter.

If your freezer space is limited or if your family doesn't want all the cuts that are part of a half or quarter, ask about buying a wholesale cut. Check the identification charts on pages 6 to 9 for information on retail cuts found in each wholesale cut.

Buying Beef in Quantity

Before you buy a beef half or quarter, consider these questions. Will your family eat all the cuts? Do you know how to prepare all the cuts? Can your budget stand the cash outlay required to buy a quarter or half? Do you have enough freezer space?

BLADE BONE · BACKBONE (T-bone) · LEG BONE · ARM BONE · RIB BONE · HIP BONES

Bone Shapes

Use the identifying bone from each area to predict the degree of tenderness. The center loin is the most tender area. Cuts become less tender closer to each end. The blade bone and round arm and leg bones indicate a need for moist-heat cooking.

Understanding Meat Labels

MEAT DEPARTMENT

WEIGHT
Lb.Net

PAY

PRICE
Per Lb.

0.00

$0.00

0.00

BEEF CHUCK
BLADE STEAK

(kind of meat)   (wholesale cut)

BEEF   **CHUCK**

(standard name for
specific cut packaged)

BLADE STEAK

As the label at right shows, the meat cut name can be broken into the following three parts: 1) the kind of meat——beef, veal, pork, lamb; 2) the whole (or primal) cut——chuck or shoulder, rib, loin, or round or leg; and 3) the retail cut—— blade roast, loin chop, etc. Learn to read the label so you'll be sure to get the exact cut you want. (If your local market hasn't adopted URMIS guidelines, encourage them to do so.)

The saying "A rose by any other name. . ." well applies to cuts of meat—a delmonico steak is a fillet steak is a beauty steak is a beef rib eye steak. And undoubtedly, like everyone else, you find all these names for the same cut very confusing.

That's why, a few years ago, the meat industry established voluntary guidelines (called Uniform Retail Meat Identity Standards, or URMIS) in an effort to standardize meat cut names throughout the country. Since these guidelines are followed in this book, if your local supermarket has also adopted them, it's easy to identify meat cuts just by looking at the label.

Inspection vs. Grading

Although inspection and grading both refer to ways of measuring meat quality, they are entirely different procedures. Meat inspection, which assures that the meat is fit for human consumption, is required by law. Grading, however, is voluntary since it deals with palatability and yield.

Every packinghouse and processing plant in the United States must meet strict requirements for the sanitation and wholesomeness of its meats. These are checked by government officials who then give carcasses a round inspection stamp.

Many beef, veal, and lamb packers also choose to have their product graded according to federal standards. These packers pay to have government employees examine each carcass and evaluate the visible characteristics that relate to tenderness, juiciness, and flavor. Only meat graded U.S. Prime, Choice, Good, or Standard is sold in retail stores, with U.S. Choice the grade most commonly available. This grading is indicated by a shield-shaped stamp on the carcass. (Pork is not graded.)

Ground Beef

What are you getting when you buy hamburger, ground beef, ground chuck, ground round, or ground sirloin? There's no one answer. Unless your store grinds under federal inspection, buys ground meat from a processor who is federally inspected, or is regulated by specific state or local laws, there is no hard and fast percentage of lean to fat for each type.

A store that uses labels with percentages of lean may be working under URMIS guidelines (see Understanding Meat Labels above). These are:

1. All ground beef should contain at least 70 percent lean. The label should read "ground beef," and state the lean-to-fat ratio as "not less than X% lean."

2. Ground beef should contain beef only and no other meat trimmings.

3. Unless labeled otherwise, ground beef should contain only skeletal meat (no variety meats).

4. A descriptive name should be used if meat is from a specific cut, i.e., ground beef chuck.

What Does Cooking Do?

Properly done, cooking improves the flavor, tenderness, and palatability of meat. To understand how it does this, we need to know a little about the composition of meat. Meat is actually skeletal muscle which is interspersed with fat and connective tissue. A large muscle, such as the eye of the round, is made up of many bundles of muscles, giving the meat a grain. These bundles are held together by connective tissue which in turn is made up of the protein collagen which is softened by cooking and the protein elastin which is not tenderized by cooking. There are two primary methods of cooking meat—— dry heat cooking and moist heat cooking.

Dry heat cooking (roasting, broiling, panbroiling, and frying): Only tender cuts of meat can satisfactorily be prepared by these methods since no moisture is added to help tenderization. Heat solidifies the protein in meat, and that's why an overdone steak may taste tough. The longer it cooks, the more solid the protein becomes, making the meat harder to chew. Overcooking or cooking at too high a temperature also increases the evaporation and loss of drippings so the meat is drier and less juicy.

Moist heat cooking (stewing, simmering, and braising): Less tender cuts of meat are usually prepared by these methods. The added moisture and long, slow cooking time help to tenderize the meat by breaking down the connective tissues so they become more gelatinous and easier to eat.

Tenderness of Meat

Tenderness depends both on the type of animal and its maturity. Lamb and pork come from younger animals so they are more naturally tender than beef. And individual cuts vary in tenderness depending on where they come from on the carcass. As a general rule, cuts from the loin area (the part of the animal that gets the least exercise) are the most tender. Tenderness tends to decrease for cuts taken farther from this area.

As you look at the meat identity charts, you'll notice that the majority of meat cuts come from the less tender areas of the animal. These cuts are usually a good buy, but how can you make them more tender?

Using moist heat cooking is the easiest way (see What Does Cooking Do? above). In addition to cooking, pounding with a meat mallet and using powdered instant meat tenderizers also help increase tenderness.

Probably the most effective home tenderizing method is to pound the meat surface with a meat mallet. This physical action breaks down some of the meat fibers. When choosing a meat mallet, make sure it's fairly heavy but comfortable to hold and swing.

Powdered instant meat tenderizers are available both seasoned and unseasoned. The main ingredient in most of them is a plant-produced enzyme that acts chemically to break down the meat protein. Be sure to follow the directions suggested for using each one.

Meat Thermometers

Timings given in recipes and roasting charts are always approximations. No two ovens cook exactly the same way, and no two roasts are shaped exactly alike or have the same amount of bone or fat. Because of these variations, a meat thermometer is your best guide to judging doneness.

To get the most accurate reading, make sure the tip of the thermometer isn't resting on bone, fat, gristle, or the bottom of the pan. Oftentimes, especially with a large roast, it's a good idea to check the temperature more than once. When the thermometer indicates the desired degree of doneness, push it into the meat a little farther. If the temperature drops, leave the roast in longer and check again.

Meat thermometers are instruments, usually needle-shaped, with a tube of mercury in the center. Prices vary depending on how well the mercury is protected.

Perfect Pan Gravy

Add special flavor to meats with browned flour gravy. In small skillet cook 1 cup all-purpose flour over medium-high heat, stirring constantly, 10 to 15 minutes or till it turns light brown. Store in covered container.

Browning flour reduces its thickening power by nearly one-half, so adjust amounts accordingly when substituting it for regular flour in gravy making.

When you're cooking a large roast in a roasting pan, it's easy to make use of those flavorful drippings by making the gravy in the pan. First, remove the meat to a warm platter and cover with foil to keep warm. Leaving the crusty bits in the pan, pour the fat and meat juices into a large liquid measuring cup. Continue as directed below, thickening either by blending with drippings or by combining with liquid.

BLEND WITH DRIPPINGS
For 2 cups gravy: Skim fat from pan juices, reserving 3 to 4 tablespoons. Return the reserved fat to the roasting pan. Blend in ¼ cup all-purpose *flour*. Place over medium heat and stir till bubbly. Add 2 cups *liquid* (pan juices plus water, milk, or broth) all at once. Cook and stir till thickened and bubbly. Season to taste with salt and pepper.

COMBINE WITH LIQUID
For 2 cups gravy: Skim fat from the pan juices. Add enough water to the pan juices to measure 1½ cups. Return juices to the roasting pan. Put ½ cup cold *water* in screw-top jar; add 2 tablespoons *cornstarch* (or ¼ cup all-purpose *flour*). Shake well. Stir into juices. Cook, stirring constantly, till mixture is thickened and bubbly. Season to taste with salt and pepper.

Basic Beef Stock

After making the broth, don't toss out the meat and bones. Use the cooked beef in soups or stews. When bones are cool, remove the meat from bones. Store meat in covered container in refrigerator or wrap in moisture-vaporproof freezer wrap; seal, label, and freeze. Makes 2 cups.

4 pounds meaty beef bones	**trimmings (approximate amounts):**
3 medium onions, quartered	**1½** cups potato peelings
1½ cups celery leaves	**1½** cups carrot peelings
6 sprigs parsley	**1½** cups turnip tops *or* peelings
4 or **5** whole peppercorns	**1½** cups parsnip tops *or* peelings (wax removed)
2 or **3** bay leaves	**4** or **5** outer leaves of cabbage
1 or **2** cloves garlic, halved	**¾** cup sliced green onion
1 tablespoon salt	**¾** cup sliced leek tops
2 teaspoons dried thyme, crushed, *or* **1** tablespoon dried basil, crushed	**1** eggshell, crushed
Use any 2 or 3 of the following vegetable	**1** egg white

In large kettle or Dutch oven combine beef bones, quartered onions, celery leaves, parsley, peppercorns, bay leaves, garlic, salt, and thyme or basil. Add 10 cups *water* and 2 or 3 of the vegetable trimmings, using only approximate measures for trimmings. Bring mixture to boiling. Cover and simmer for 2½ to 3 hours.

Using slotted spoon, remove meat and bones (use as directed in note, left). Strain stock, discarding vegetables and herbs. To clarify stock, combine eggshell, egg white, and ¼ cup *water*. Stir into hot stock; bring to boiling. Remove from heat; let stand 5 minutes.

Strain stock through a double thickness of cheesecloth. Skim off excess fat or chill and lift off the fat. Pour stock into pint or quart jars or containers; cover and chill. (Store stock in refrigerator up to 2 weeks or in freezer up to 6 months.) Use stock in any recipe that calls for broth, or serve alone. Makes 7 to 8 cups.

Storage

Keep meat at its best by protecting against spoilage with proper care and storage. Bring meat home and place in the refrigerator or freezer as soon as possible.

Fresh meat purchased pre-cut and wrapped in clear flexible packaging may be refrigerated as purchased. If it is to be frozen, remove the clear packaging material and tightly wrap the meat in moisture-vaporproof freezer paper. (See Wrapping Meat for the Freezer, below.)

Occasionally check the temperature of your refrigerator meat keeper. It should be between 36° and 40°F. Upright or chest freezers and refrigerator-freezers should maintain 0°F. or lower.

Maximum Meat Storage Times

Safeguard your meat against spoilage with proper handling and storage. Preventing potentially dangerous bacterial growth on meat is mostly a matter of avoiding exposure to warm temperatures and improper wrapping. Always purchase meat that's sealed tightly and feels cold.

Keep the working areas clean by scrubbing cutting boards and utensils with hot soapy water before and after each use. Diluted bleach also helps clean up wooden cutting boards. This is very important because bacteria can be transmitted from an unwashed cutting board to the meat.

MEAT	REFRIGERATOR (36° to 40°F.)	FREEZER (0° or lower)
BEEF		
Roasts	2 to 4 days	6 to 12 months
Steaks	2 to 4 days	6 to 12 months
Ground Beef, Stew Meat	1 to 2 days	3 to 4 months
PORK		
Roasts (fresh)	2 to 4 days	3 to 6 months
Chops, Spareribs (fresh)	2 to 4 days	3 to 6 months
Ground Pork	1 to 2 days	1 to 3 months
Hams, Picnics (whole)	7 days	2 months
Bacon	5 to 7 days	1 month
VEAL		
Roasts	2 to 4 days	6 to 9 months
Chops	2 to 4 days	6 to 9 months
LAMB		
Roasts	2 to 4 days	6 to 9 months
Chops	2 to 4 days	6 to 9 months
Ground Lamb	1 to 2 days	3 to 4 months
VARIETY MEATS	1 to 2 days	3 to 4 months
COOKED MEATS	4 to 5 days	2 to 3 months

Wrapping Meat for the Freezer

Properly wrapping meat helps assure against dehydration (freezer burn). Use wrapping 1½ times as long as needed to go around meat. Place meat in the center. The coated side of the wrapping paper should be next to the meat. Bring sides of wrapping together at the top. Fold edges down in a series of locked folds. Press wrapping securely against the meat. Crease the ends of wrapping into points. Press wrapping to remove pockets of air. Bring both ends of the wrapping together at the top. Secure ends with some freezer tape. Label package with the contents and the date.

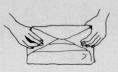

Meat Carving

Carving meat can be baffling, especially when it comes to slicing all types of meat cuts. To carve meat successfully, keep the knife's cutting edge very sharp. For best results, sharpen knives with a hand-held sharpening steel or stone before each use. With steel or stone in one hand, hold knife in the other hand at a 20° angle to the sharpener. Draw the blade edge over the sharpener, using a motion that goes across and down at the same time. Turn blade over, reverse directions, and sharpen other side, an equal number of times.

To keep knives clean, wipe them with a wet cloth after each use, then dry. And, to keep knives in good condition, proper storage is essential. Keep knives separated, either in a holder or in a rack, to prevent them from becoming blunted.

Beef Rib Roast

Carving the rib roast is easier if the chine bone (part of backbone) is removed and the rib bones are cut short by the meatman. Place rib roast on warm platter with largest end down. This forms a solid base for carving. Insert carving fork

between top two ribs. Starting on fat side of the piece of meat, slice across the meat to rib bone. Use tip of knife to cut along rib bone to

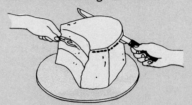

loosen each slice, if whole rib is not served. Keep as close to rib bones as possible, making the largest serving of meat.

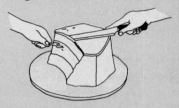

Beef Flank Steak

Place the flank steak on a wooden cutting board, holding the meat steady on the board with the carving fork. With the narrow end of the steak to carver's right, begin slicing. With the knife blade at an

angle parallel to board, cut the meat in very thin slices all at the same

angle. Carving this way cuts with the grain of the flank steak.

Crown Roast

Crown roast should have all of the center stuffing removed before carving. Using fork to steady, start carving where ribs are tied. Cut between ribs. Remove to plate.

Beef brisket is sliced at an angle across the grain, ⅛ to ¼ inch thick. Carve from two sides since the grain goes in several directions.

Beef Brisket

Leg of Lamb

With shank on carver's right, cut 2 or 3 slices from thin side parallel to leg bone; turn leg to rest on this base. Steady with carving fork. Beginning at shank end, cut ¼-inch slices down to leg bone. Continue cutting till bone pointing upward is reached. With fork still in place, start at shank end and cut along leg bone to release slices. Tip roast on side to carve the remaining meat.

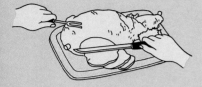
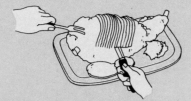
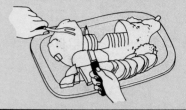

Beef Porterhouse Steak

Place steak on cutting board. Hold steak steady with a carving fork. Using the tip of knife, start at the top of the T-shaped bone and cut down and around to the bottom of bone. Start at the top of the bone on the other side and cut around to the bottom. Lift out the bone and discard. Slice across the full width of steak, cutting through the top loin and tenderloin muscles. Trim off fat and discard. For thick steaks, diagonal slicing rather than crosswise slicing is recommended.

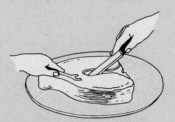

Shank Half of Ham

With shank at the carver's left, turn ham so that the thick cushion side is up. Steady ham with carving fork. Using sharp knife, cut along the top of the leg and the shank bones and under fork to lift off the boneless cushion. Remove the cushion and place it on a cutting board. Cut perpendicular slices, as shown. Cut around the leg bone with the tip of the knife to remove any meat from this bone. Turn meat so that the broadest side is down. Cut perpendicular slices in same manner as the boneless cushion piece.

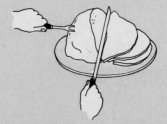
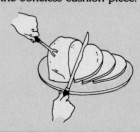

Beef Chuck Blade Pot Roast

Place pot roast on cutting board. Steady meat with carving fork. Trim away any excess fat. Cut between the muscles and around the bones to remove one solid section of roast at a time. Turn section just removed so meat fibers are parallel to board. This makes it possible to carve across the grain of meat. Cut the slices about ¼ inch thick.

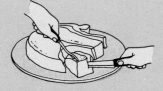

Index

Index